I0051806

BOOKKEEPING MANAGEMENT

Ed Wuensche

The information in this book is the opinion of the author. The author is not responsible for any decisions made based on the information in this book.

Copyright 2017 Edwin Wuensche

All rights reserved. The text of this publication, or any part thereof, may not be reproduced in any manner whatsoever without the written permission of the author.

Portion of the author's previous copyrighted books (Bookkeeping Journey & Bookkeeping Management Journey) are included in this book.

ISBN 978-0-692-95199-6

Design book cover-Ellen Wuensche
Illustrate cover picture-Ellen Wuensche

TABLE OF CONTENTS

ACKNOWLEDGEMENT

I am blessed to be married to Sandy. I dedicate the writing of this book to her. Thanks to Sandy Wuensche for editing the book and for making suggestions that were very useful.

Matthew Wuensche reviewed the book. His main contribution was providing input for clarity to the reader and for those individuals with limited or no financial background. He also reviewed for conformity of text presentation.

He set up the following web sites:

www.bookkeepingmanagement.com
www.edwuensche.com
www.sb-help.com (note the dash)

Ellen Wuensche designed and created the cover of this book. She met the technical requirement of submitting online the completed manuscript and covers for printing. Technical support and some clarity to the Fast Track Learning sections was also provided by her.

It takes much education and knowledge to be a CPA (Certified Public Accountants). **However, it does not require any financial education or experience to understand the CPA's financial statements (Income Statement & Balance Sheet) when you read this book.**

The first two sections: *Fast Track Income Statement Learning & Fast Tract Balance Sheet Learning* give understanding so you can manage from those statements. Instructive information coupled with examples fosters simple learning. You will be surprised how easy it is.

Clients stories backing up a pitfall, tip, or other information is an interesting and pertinent part of this book.

Many other topics (listed in the index) relate to management or general information and are discussed often with an example for easy comprehension.

After reading this book, you will be equipped with financial knowledge to manage your own business or you will either be able to converse in a meeting of your organization, business setting, or even in a business classroom.

For over 45 years, I have been blessed to be able to work for many small business clients including startups giving them monthly financial statements and providing other needed help. With so many clients over so many years and watching their decision making, I have seen the pattern of how successful startups and existing business operate.

Anyone can become financial statement competent without regard to education or experience. The nutshell is knowing what financial information to use to manage the business or organization and avoiding the crippling pitfalls.

FAST TRACK

INCOME STATEMENT

LEARNING

Information below refers to next page:

Note that an INCOME STATEMENT is divided into 5 parts*

A) **SALES PRICE or INCOME** This is income for selling a product or providing a service or other miscellaneous income.

B) **COST** of the **product sold or COST of providing the service.**

C) **GROSS PROFIT – A minus B** This is the profit on the sale of products or services before operating expenses are deducted.

D) **OPERATING EXPENSES - Expenses other than B** These are the costs to operate the business. These costs are not the product costs or service costs.

E) **NET PROFIT - A minus B & D or C-D** This is your total sales or income minus all your costs.

*Organizations, etc. that do not sell products or services will not have **B** above. They will have **A, D, E** as in the following examples.

Income Statement divided into 5 parts

Example:

Sale-One bushel of apples- $200.00
Cost of bushel of apples--- $120.00

Operating expenses:
Rent of market stall --------- $ 23.00

A) Sales (Income) $200.00

B) Cost of Goods Sold $120.00

C) GROSS PROFIT $ 80.00

D) Operating Expenses $ 23.00

E) Net Income $ 57.00

Information below refers to next page:

The following pages will show different types of businesses with different **B** costs.

INCOME STATEMENT - LEMONADE STAND
   (similar to manufacturing business)

MANUFACTURING-Cost of Goods Manufactured

COSTS: All costs necessary to manufacture the products
Example: Computer manufacturing and any business that starts with materials to produce a product. To simplify, expense such as rent not allocated for space used in manufacturing.

B) Total cost to MAKE lemonade (lemons, sugar, water, labor and supplies) is $90.00.
   B only includes the purchasing costs and labor cost and other directly related expenses of making lemonade.

D) Labor to SELL lemonade is $90.00, which is *part* of **total operating expenses**.
   This labor was not part of the cost of making the lemonade but to sell the lemonade.

 Without an Income Statement, the owner would not realize that the company lost money. After analyzing the sales and the expenses, the owner can now make adjustments to turn that loss into a profit.

INCOME STATEMENT – MANUFACTURING BUSINESS

Lemonade Stand Income Statement

7/1/xx to 7/31/xx

A) Sales/Income $300.00 100.0%

Minus:
Lemons $ 15.00
Sugar   17.00
Water   4.00
Labor (to make lemonade)   40.00
Payroll Taxes   4.00
Supplies   10.00
B) Total Cost of Sales* $ 90.00 30.0%

C) Gross Profit $210.00 70.0%

Minus:
Operating Expenses:
Advertising $125.00
Rent   100.00
Labor (to sell lemonade)   90.00
Payroll Tax   9.00
D) Total Operating Expenses $324.00 108.0%

E Net Profit (Loss) $(114.00) (38.00%)

The importance of the % will be discussed later.
* Manufacturing- would be Cost of Goods Manufactured.

Information below refers to next page:

INCOME STATEMENT – SERVICE BUSINESS
(delivery services and other businesses offering only service)

Cost of Operations would replace **B** on previous page.
COSTS: Salary, Contract Labor and any related costs for performing the service such as Employee Benefits and Vehicle Expenses.

The Cost of Operations includes all costs to provide that service.

The **Labor Costs** means every labor cost involved in providing the service including payroll taxes and benefits, like health insurance, for those workers.

Transportation costs includes gas, vehicle repairs, etc. for a delivery service or a similar business.

Operating expenses:

Salary-office includes only salaries of office personnel, not directly related to providing the services, such as a secretary or accountant. Other possible Operating Expenses and explanations are listed and discussed on **pages 10-25**.

.

6

INCOME STATEMENT – SERVICE BUSINESS

A) Income---------------------------- $1,300.00 100.0%

Minus:

Salary (labor)	$ 500.00	
Payroll Taxes	50.00	
Health Insurance	100.00	
Vehicle – gas	150.00	
Vehicle – repair	50.00	
B) Total Cost of Operations	**$ 850.00**	**65.4%**

C) Gross Income $ 450.00 34.6%

Minus:

Operating Expenses:

Rent	$ 150.00	
Office	100.00	
Payroll Taxes	10.00	
Salary-office	100.00	
D) Total Operating Expenses	**$ 360.00**	**27.7%**

E) Net Profit $ 90.00   6.9%

Information below refers to next page:

INCOME STATEMENT – SERVICE & PARTS
(auto repair, computer repair, and any other business offering services and necessary parts to complete the job)

Cost of Operations would replace **B** in manufacturing business example.
COSTS: service costs plus parts costs

B) COST OF OPERATIONS:
Includes all the labor, parts and other costs
to fix autos ,etc.

Includes payroll taxes and other costs such as health insurance.

Gas and vehicles costs are also included if used in business.
Example: Picking up parts from the parts house.

D) OPERATING EXPENSES:

Salary includes only salaries not directly
related to providing the services such as
office salary.

Other possible Operating Expenses and explanations are listed and discussed on **pages 10-25**.

INCOME STATEMENT – SERVICE & PARTS

A) Income $ 3,000.00 100.0%

Minus:
Salary (labor) $ 1,000.00
Parts 750.00
Payroll Taxes 90.00
B) Total Cost of Operations $1,840.00 61.3%

C) GROSS PROFIT $1,160.00 38.7%

Minus:
Operating Expenses:
Rent $ 350.00
Office 100.00
Salary-Office 300.00
Payroll Taxes 31.50

D) Total Operating Expenses $ 781.50 26.1%

E) Net Income $ 378.50 12.6%

INCOME STATEMENT – RETAIL (EXPANDED AC-COUNTS)

(grocery stores, any business that sells products)

Cost of Goods Sold replaces **B** in manufacturing business example.

PRESENTING A MORE DETAILED INCOME STATEMENT

March 1
to
March 31

A- INCOME:

A-1 Sales $ 10,000.00 100.0%

B- COST OF GOODS SOLD:

B-1 Beginning Inventory	$ 1,000.00	
B-2 Purchases	9,000.00	
B-3 Total Goods Available for Sale	10,000.00	
B-4 (-) Ending Inventory	2,000.00	
B-5 COST OF GOODS SOLD	$ 8,000.00	80.0%
C- GROSS PROFIT	$ 2,000.00	20.0%

D- OPERATING EXPENSES:

D-1 Advertising	$ 22.00	.2%
D-2 Amortization	10.00	.1
D-3 Bad Debt	14.00	.1
D-4 Bank Service Charge	10.00	.1
D-5 Computer Expenses	78.00	.8
D-6 Contribution	10.00	.1

D-7 Depreciation	240.00	2.4
D-8 Entertainment	25.00	.3
D-9 FICA Expenses	76.50	.7
D-10 Fringe Benefits	25.00	.3
D-11 Garbage Disposal	40.00	.4
D-12 Insurance	118.33	1.2
D-13 Interest	25.00	.3
D-14 Legal	40.00	.4
D-15 Licenses, Fees, Permits	10.00	.1
D-16 Maintenance and Repairs	27.00	.3
D-17 Miscellaneous	55.00	.5
D-18 Office Expense	24.00	.2
D-19 Professional Expense	190.00	1.9
D-20 Rent	400.00	4.0
D-21 Salary	1000.00	10.0
D-22 Security	35.00	.4
D-23 Store Supplies	150.00	1.5
D-24 Taxes-FUTA-SUTA	16.80	.2

D-25 Taxes-Property-Other	0	
D-26 Telephone	42.00	.4
D-27 Travel	184.00	1.8
D-28 Truck-Auto Expense	136.00	1.4
D-29 Utilities	72.00	.7
D-30_____		
D-31_____		
D-32 TOTAL OPERATING EXPENSES	$ 3075.63	30.8%

E- NET PROFIT or INCOME (loss)   ($ 1075.63) (10.8%)

Note that each of the accounts above are discussed in detail on pages 13 – 25.

D) OPERATING EXPENSES, an explanation: (refers to pages 10 & 11)

Tax rules can change at any time. Check current tax laws before relying on any of the tax information given.

OPERATING EXPENSES DETAIL:

D-1 Advertising: (See D-1 on page 10)
Advertising is an expense made for the purpose of increasing sales. Each type of business has various options in an advertising program such as newspaper, radio, television, direct selling, internet, etc. The options should be analyzed to determine which form of advertising will have the greater effect on net profit per dollar spent. Each customer invoice could indicate the source of advertising that created the sale, such as newspaper, internet sources, and yellow pages.

D-2 Amortization:
Amortization is a bookkeeping entry for a previous improvement expenditure that has a life of more than one month. The $10.00 shown on the income statement was computed as follows:

New carpet for the office at a cost of $600.00 was bought on January 1. The carpet improvement will last as long as the office lease of 5 years (60 months). The monthly amortization for your income statement will be computed as follows:

$$\frac{\$600.00 \text{ cost of carpet}}{60 \text{ months}} = \$10.00 \text{ per month}$$

D-3 Bad Debts:

A bad debt is also a bookkeeping entry. As soon as it is certain that you will not be paid the amount due from a customer (**Accounts Receivable**), or a returned check, etc., it is charged to bad debt expense.

John Will's $14.00 check to your company was deposited into the bank and returned to you. You are unable to collect the amount of the check from him. The bad debt is $14.00.
If the total amount of your bad debts is large, investigate to determine the reason. Review your extension of credit and your collection policies and methods. Are they consistent and are they efficient?

D-4 Bank Service Charge:

Bank service charges are charges by banks for their services (other than interest).

D-5 Computer Expenses:

These are expenses like computer repairs, expenses other than hardware (computers).

D-6 Contribution:

Contributions are usually a deductible expense (a reduction in income) for a C corporation, up to 10% of net income when made to a qualified non-profit entity. Contributions of an individually owned business and other entities may be deductions on the personal tax return of its owner(s). Congress could change these laws.

Be aware of the portion of your donation that the intended recipients actually receive, especially for an organization that you are not familiar with. It varies greatly from organization to organization according to their respective **overhead expenses.** Maybe you can find out from the Better Business Bureau, or another information source, about the % of the contributions spent on overhead. In some cases only a part of your contributions is used for its primary goal, the rest on salaries and overhead of the non-profit organization.

D-7 Depreciation:
Depreciation is the expense allocated each month, for a certain portion of the cost of fixed assets. Depreciation is not money that you pay out, but only a bookkeeping entry based on the cost of the asset.

Note the balance sheet on pages **60-61.** It shows all of the assets including fixed assets such as furniture & fixtures, trucks, equipment etc. An Allowance for Depreciation amount is also shown. The depreciation expense is computed as follows:

Truck – estimated 5 years or 60 months
Equipment – estimated 7 years or 84 months of functional use

$\dfrac{\$6,000.00 \text{ truck cost}}{60 \text{ months life}}$ = $100.00 per month

$\dfrac{\$11,760.00 \text{ equipment}}{84 \text{ months life}}$ = $140.00 per month

Total depreciation for statement $240.00 per month

D-8 Entertainment:
These are the expenditures you make to entertain present or potential customers and customer contacts.

For management purposes, you should keep a record of who made the contact and the increase in business, if any, as a result of the expense. By examining these figures over a period of months, you will be able to identify which employee's entertainment expenditures increased your gross profit figure.
If you get **audited** by the Internal Revenue Service, you may have to furnish receipts and information showing: the date, the payee, amount of the bill, and what business was discussed.

D-9 FICA Expenses:
The amount of social security taxes (FICA) withheld from employee's salary, including corporate officers, is matched by the employer. The matching amount is your FICA expense.

This tax is payable at a fixed rate on all employee's salary up to a salary limit set by Social Security. For the year of 2017, the Social Security rate is 6.2% each for employee and employer or 12.4% total up to the $127,200.00 salary limit. The Medicare tax rate is 1.45% each for employee and employer or 2.9% total and is payable on all salary amounts. An additional Medicare tax of .009 is due on earned income above a certain amount.

Owners of an unincorporated business pay 15.3% for this tax and take a deduction of ½ of this self-employment tax on their personal tax return.

D-10 Fringe Benefits:
This can include office and officer's employee health insurance and other small benefits for employees. A separate account for health insurance could be made apart from fringe benefits. Health insurance costs vary widely.

D-11 Garbage Disposal:
Garbage Disposal is an expense for hauling away or disposing of trash. It may be done by a private or public company.

D-12 Insurance:
Insurance is an expense that allows you a recovery for casualty damage liability, claim by an injured party, etc. There are many types of insurance.

When the insurance is prepaid for months ahead, the allocation of the expense is a bookkeeping entry. In such cases it is only an expense for the current period to the extent that it is used during that time. The unused portion is an asset titled *prepaid insurance*.

The income statement (p10-11) shows $118.33 as an expense for 3 types of insurance (including Liability Ins.):

Liability insurance, costing $300.00, was paid 1 year in advance—1/12 of the $300.00 is an expense for the current period ----
-------------------------------------- **$ 25.00**

Truck insurance, costing $200.00, was paid for 6 months in advance—1/6 of the $200.00 is an expense for the current period ---
------------------------------------- **33.33**

Workmen's Compensation insurance is paid on a monthly basis. If the money you owe for one month is paid in a following month, the expense is recorded in the month in which it is owed. In this case, it is computed as follows:

Example
Salary: Rate charged by insurance company:

$6.00 per $100.00 salary of $1000.00   1000/100=10

10 x $6.00 per $100.00 salary = **60.00**
Total Insurance   **$118.33**

The Workmen's Compensation (for injured employees) rate that a company pays for an office worker is much lower than what is paid for a production worker. **Business Interruption Insurance**, not included in this example, replaces lost net profit if your business is shut down because of fire, etc. It is worthy of mention here because it can be very useful, providing money to pay fixed expenses when there is no income.

Management should study the types of insurance available to decide which best meets its needs. The decision should be based on legal requirements, costs, and risk exposure. Note that deductibles (amount of money you agree to pay before the insurance company pays) can have a big effect on the cost of your insurance.

D-13 Interest:

Interest is a charge for the use of someone else's money and can be computed several ways. The interest is computed on the principal balance. Is the interest fixed or subject to fluctuation and how much?

Simple interest is figured by multiplying the principal balance on the date of computation by the interest rate for the period of the loan. ($1,000.00 x 8% x 1 year = $80.00). Payments made during the term of the loan reduce the interest you owe.

The *effective rate of interest* is the actual interest you are paying and is now required by law to be shown on all loans.

The $25.00 shown as interest on the income statement on page **11** was computed as follows:

A loan for $3,000.00 @ 10% interest for 1 years equals $300.00 interest. The monthly interest expense is:

$$\frac{\$300.00}{12} \quad = \quad \$25.00$$

Today many loans are tied to a certain loan rate. When that rate goes up or down, your interest rate is adjusted accordingly.

You can establish a *line of credit* with banks, etc. so that when your business needs immediate cash, it will be available. A line of credit with a bank is the ability to borrow up to a certain amount of cash when needed. You can then continually borrow and pay back at your discretion.

Some firms *factor their receivables*. That means they either continually sell their *receivables* (amount owed the company for sales) to the factoring company or use their receivables as security for the loan. The company or the factoring company, according to the agreement, collects the receivables.

D-14 Legal Expenses:

Legal fees are usually necessary expenses for businesses. You may want your attorney to indicate what the total cost of his service to you will be before he renders any legal services. Sometimes that is hard for him to do; however, an estimate should help insure against big expense surprises. See page **126-127** for brief management information that may be useful to manage attorney fees

D-15 Licenses, Fees, Permits:

Expenditures for licenses, permits, and the payment of other fees are required by government for some business operations and for the commencement of special work in particular locations.

Building codes might require certain permits before a building can be built or used for business. This can create problems if the starting business is unable to occupy the building until these unplanned expenditures are met.

D-16 Maintenance and Repairs:

These are minor repairs and general maintenance costs.

D-17 Miscellaneous:

There are frequently small expenditures that do not fall into any of the other categories on the Income Statement. These may be classified as Miscellaneous.

D-18 Office Expense:

These are the various office expenses such as paper supplies, etc. In small offices with no purchasing departments, businesses can often reduce their office expense by putting one responsible person in charge of all purchases for the office.

D-19 Professional Expense:

These are professional expenses like consulting, etc. You may hire someone that can help you with a particular problem.

D-20 Rent:
This is the amount of money you pay for the use of space in a building or use of property. Your rental agreement may include other expenses such as utilities, taxes, etc.

One of my clients at a retail location signed a 10 year lease. A sizable competitor moved nearby resulting in monthly losses for my client's business. If his lease contract had not had a defect, his business would have taken a big hit.

After that, he would sign 5 two year lease contracts with options to renew after 2 years. In other words, he would have the option to renew the contract every 2 years 4 times. However, having such a contract depends on the leasing company.

D-21 Salary:
All salary paid to employees is lumped under "salary" in this example. There could be a separate heading for each department or job classification.

> Example:
> Salary-Clerical

Note: If your business is a corporation, set up a separate account like "Salary-Officer" for any officer's salary. As mentioned before, the owner of an unincorporated business does not record any salary for himself. He pays his income tax on his business profits.

D-22 Security:
Alarm Protection, for the purpose of preventing or detecting theft, is one of the most common types of security expense for a retail business. There are many other types of security expenses such as shopping services, cameras, guards, dogs, etc.

Cameras strategically placed, where the customer is checked out or where inventory is stored, can be very helpful. Cameras can record checkers, who don't ring up some or all of their friends' purchases, or monitor inventory movement to prevent employee theft.

D-23 Store Supplies:
These are supplies such as trash bags, etc., bought for the operation of the store but not for resale.

D-24 Taxes-FUTA-SUTA:
These are the payroll amounts paid to your State Employment Commission (SUTA) and the Internal Revenue Service (FUTA) as unemployment taxes. Your SUTA tax is low when former employees do not draw unemployment compensation and can be high when they do.

Since the SUTA tax payment can vary greatly depending on your tax rate, be aware of your rights as an employer. Note that it may help your case to prevent an increase in the tax rate by documenting any employee abuses. You can then use those documents to contest an employee charge to your account that would result in a rate increase to the employer. Check with your state employment commission. The $16.80 shown on page 11 was owed for federal and state unemployment taxes. The FUTA tax is based on payroll.

D-25 Taxes-Property-Other
Property taxes including any other state and local taxes--does not include income taxes.

D-26 Telephone:

This is the expense for the use of your telephone including long distance calls. Cell phone costs can be included here or you could set up a separate account for cell phone expenses.

D-27 Travel:

This is the expense of traveling for business purposes. It includes transportation costs, hotels, food, etc.

D-28 Truck-Auto Expense:

These are expenses for vehicle repairs and gasoline. For more detailed management information, you could have an account for "gas" and a separate account for "auto-truck repairs", etc. This expense is for salesmen, executives, whoever; it is not the direct cost of earning your income.

Charges against this expense should be checked periodically, especially when the expenditure is excessive. It is helpful to keep a record of the amount each employee spends in this area.

D-29 Utilities:

This is the expenditure for electricity, gas, and water. For some types of businesses, these expenditures can be large.

D-30, 31

Use these lines to list any expenses not listed above.

D-32 Total Operating Expenses:

This is the total of all operating expenses **(D-1 through D-31)**.

COMMENTARY

Special things you need to know
to fill out the Operating Expense section:

1) Purchase of a truck, equipment, adding machine, etc. is not an expense but an asset. However, a certain percent of the cost is *depreciation expense* **(D-7) page 11. See page 15** for details.

2) Payment on notes or loans is not an Operating Expense. It is a reduction of the Notes Payable on the Balance Sheet **(B-6) page 61.** However, the interest portion is deductible as an *interest expense* **(D-13) page 11. See page 18** for details.

3) Withholding & FICA taxes, those withheld from the employee's check, are not Operating Expenses but payment of a liability **(B-2) page 61.** However the matching FICA tax is an expense **(D-9), page11. See pages 15-16** for details.

4) Any expense that is paid for more than one month in the future (prepaid expense) is not fully an expense for that month. Only the amount or percent of the cost pertaining to that month is an expense. Insurance and Interest are two common *prepaid expenses* amortized each month.**(D-12 & D-13), page 11. See pages 16-18** for details.

Similar expenses can be lumped into one category expense, like Insurance, or listed separately as items in that category. For example, the Insurance category can be divided into, truck insurance, liability insurance, Workmen's Compensation insurance, theft insurance, etc.

ANALYZING OPERATING EXPENSES
FOR MANAGEMENT PURPOSES

Management should analyze each expense and ask:

1) Is this expense necessary? Will profits be reduced in the short term and/or long term if this expenditure is made? Your profit will be greater initially if an outlay, such as Advertising, is not made. But over the long term, your profits may be less if you don't make that expenditure.

2) If an expenditure is necessary ask, "Am I getting the most value for the money spent?" This pertains to most types of expenditures. At the beginning, if you are not well capitalized, avoid paying for frills that are not essential for the operation of the business.

3) Are there alternatives to present expenditures which afford the same benefit?

4) In absentee ownership (though many companies may find it beneficial to have a budgeted income statement), budgets may be prepared and department heads held responsible for the expenditures. Good management control, through explicit delegation of responsibilities, helps to prevent abuse in expense areas such as entertainment, auto, travel, etc. Once decisions are made and responsibilities are delegated, do I have effective means of control?

Each expense should be analyzed separately. If sales are fairly stable from one month to the next, the monthly percent of each of these Operating Expenses can be compared to the year-to-date *expense percent*. An expense percent figure is the total expense of the item divided by its sales.

Example: $\dfrac{\text{rent payments of } \$1{,}200.00}{\$40{,}000.00 \text{ sales}}$ = 3.0%

The owner of a small business is usually conscious of each amount spent. As the business grows, there is sometimes a tendency not to watch these Operating Expenses as carefully as before. The goal of getting the most for each dollar spent is overlooked.

You can see which percentages are above or below your normal average and then analyze the situation thoroughly. On the Income Statement for the month of March, a loss of $1075.63 was reported. See page **11**. It is important that you have such information as soon as possible after the month ends, so you can determine if your Net Income is lower than projected and, if so, hopefully correct it by the following month.

It is much easier to control your Operating Expenses than it is to control the Gross Profit and the Gross Profit Percent (will be discussed beginning next page). To control Gross Profit and Gross Profit Percent, you have to effectively manage three variables: Sales, Purchases, and Inventory. It is often hard to pinpoint which variable is causing a low Gross Profit and Gross Profit Percent. To control Operating Expenses, you have to decide which expenditures are necessary. Then make certain that only those expenditures are made.

If you have a budgeted Income Statement, you would compare your actual expense amount with the budgeted amount for that expense for that month. If there is a difference, the activity for that expense account can be checked. With the *accounting* software of today, it is easy to set budgeted financial statements.

GROSS PROFIT & GROSS PROFIT %
(See page 10)

Sales	$10,000.00	100.0%
Minus:		
Cost of Goods Sold (Retail)	$ 8,000.00	80.0%
GROSS PROFIT	$ 2,000.00	20.0%

Gross Profit equals Sales less Cost of Goods Sold (retail) or Cost of Operations (service) or Cost of Goods Manufactured (manufacturing).

The Gross Profit % is Gross Profit divided by Sales.

The reason the Gross Profit % is so important is that when it varies from your projected goal, you know something caused it. It is especially important for the beginning retail business to manage the Gross Profit and Gross Profit % in order to reach profit goals.

Often a service type business, with different bid Gross Profit %s, will look at the Net Income first. If that does not meet projections, they first look at their bidding process.

GROSS PROFIT %

GROSS PROFIT % IS PROBABLY THE MOST IMPORTANT MANAGEMENT % ON THE INCOME STATEMENT.

The Gross Profit % is computed by dividing Gross Profit ($2,000.00) by Sales ($10,000.00). $2,000.00 divided by $10,000.00 = 20.0%

IF YOUR INCOME STATEMENT DOES NOT MEET YOUR PROJECTED GROSS PROFIT %, YOU HAVE A MANAGEMENT ISSUE.

GOOD MANAGEMENT WILL IMMEDIATELY TRY TO ISOLATE THE PROBLEM (Sales, Purchases or Inventory) AND FIX IT.

The example shows that an increased Gross Profit % from 20% (Business A) to 40% (Business B) results in a $2,000.00 higher Gross Profit (Business B).

Business B's Net Income is a $2,000.00 increase over Business A's $0.00 Net Income.

Operating Expenses of both businesses remained the same.

GROSS PROFIT %

Business A		Business B	
Sales			
$10,000.00	100.0%	$10,000.00	100.0%
Cost of Goods Sold or Cost of Operations			
$ 8,000.00	80.0%	$ 6,000.00	60.0%
Gross Profit			
$ 2,000.00	20.0%	$ 4,000.00	40.0%
Operating Expenses			
$ 2,000.00	20.0%	$ 2,000.00	20.0%
Net Income			
$ 0	0.0%	$ 2,000.00	20.0%

INVENTORY EFFECT

ON

GROSS PROFIT

You have completed your bookkeeping for the month which shows your net income of $1,000.00.

An accountant could increase, with no evidence, your profit by showing a bigger amount for inventory.

An inventory increase from $1,000.00 to $3,000.00 would increase net income from $1,000.00 to $3,000.00.

Beware - Businesses!

Inventory below refers to next page:

INVENTORY EFFECT ON GROSS PROFIT

Inventory is the items purchased or manufactured not sold and available for sale. When all the numbers, except Inventory, have been calculated in Cost of Goods, the Inventory number can make a big difference in Gross Profit and therefore Net Income.

Inventory can be manipulated to show a higher than actual amount. Therefore partners, bankers, and investors, that have a financial interest, need to pay attention to how the Inventory is calculated. The business might actually be losing money, but an increased bogus Inventory number creates an inflated bogus profit.

An example of how Income can be increased just by increasing the Inventory:

The ending Inventory was increased from $2,000.00 to $4,000.00 and $6,000.00. Notice the Gross Profit was increased from $1,000.00 to $3,000.00 and to $5,000.00.

A warning:
Inventory can be increased just to show more profit without any evidence for it. An unwarranted bookkeeping entry can easily be made into the bookkeeping records to increase Inventory.

A question could be asked if the increase in Profit is due to an increase in Inventory.

When an entry is made by the accountant to increase Inventory, the Profit increases by the amount of the Inventory increase. The reverse is true. Individuals receiving the Income Statement need to be aware **of a possible unwarranted Inventory number.**

INVENTORY EFFECT ON GROSS PROFIT

When all the numbers, except Inventory, have been calculated in Cost of Goods, the inventory number can make a big difference in Gross Profit and therefore Net Income.

The business might actually be losing money, but an increased bogus inventory number creates an inflated bogus profit.

	Business A	Unwarranted Adjustment	Unwarranted Adjustment
A) Sales	$15,000.00	$15,000.00	$15,000.00
Beginning Inventory	$ 5,000.00	$ 5,000.00	$ 5,000.00
Purchases	11,000.00	11,000.00	11,000.00
Total	$16,000.00	$16,000.00	$16,000.00
Minus: Ending Inventory	$ 2,000.00	$ 4,000.00	$ 6,000.00
B) Cost of Goods Sold	$14,000.00	$12,000.00	$10,000.00
A-B=C C) Gross Profit	$ 1,000.00	$ 3,000.00	$ 5,000.00

When ending Inventory increases, Gross Profit increases.
When ending Inventory decreases, Gross Profit decreases.

DOUBLE SALES

MAY MORE THAN DOUBLE

NET INCOME

This is management's goal: Assuming you have reached your Gross Profit % goal.
Keep the same or greater Gross Profit % with the same or more sales and keep Operating Expenses the same.

Gross Profit - Operating Exp. = Net Income.

	A		B	
Sales	**$1,000.00**	**100.0%**	**$2,000.00**	**100.0%**
Minus:				
Cost of Goods Sold	$ 700.00		$1,400.00	
Gross Profit	**$ 300.00**	**30.0%**	**$ 600.00**	**30.0%**
Minus:				
Operating Expenses	$ 200.00	--Same--	$ 200.00	
Net Income	**$ 100.00**		**$ 400.00**	

Rather than Net Income increasing from $100.00 to $200.00 with the doubling of sales and operating expenses remaining the same, Net Income was $400.00.

This is why management oriented financial statements are so important. You continually monitor and manage.

Information below refers to next page:

DOUBLE SALES MAY MORE THAN DOUBLE NET PROFIT

The Sales doubled from $16,000.00 to $32,000.00.

The Gross Profit % remained the same at 25.0%.

Operating Expenses remained at $1,500.00.

The profit on the $16,000.00 sales was $2,500.00.
If you doubled the sales to $32,000.00, the profit
being doubled would be $5,000.00.

However the profits were more than doubled to $6,500.00.

When you can keep the Gross Profit %, 25.0% in this case, and
Operating Expenses the same ($1,500.00), while increasing
Sales, you can more than double your Net Profit.

Every Gross Profit % amount of sales then goes directly to your
Net Income.

DOUBLE SALES MAY MORE THAN DOUBLE NET INCOME

	Projection A		Projection B	
A) Sales	$16,000.00	**100.0%**	$32,000.00	**100.0%**
B) Cost of Sales	$12,000.00	**75.0%**	$ 24,000.00	**75.0%**
A-B=C C) Gross Profit %	$ 4,000.00	**25.0%**	$8,000.00	**25.0%**
D) Operating Expenses	$1,500.00	9.4%	$1,500.00	4.7%
C-D=E E) Net Income (Profit)	$ 2,500.00	15.6%	$ 6,500.00	20.3%

DIFFERENCES IN GROSS PROFIT %

AND

OPERATING EXPENSES

This shows what happens when both Gross Profit %s and Operating Expenses differ. The net income can vary wildly.

Monitor and Manage

Information below refers to next page:

DIFFERENCES IN GROSS PROFIT % AND OPERATING EXPENSES

Note that the sales were the same. Gross Profit % and Operating Expenses vary. Net Income is different.

Every business's Gross Profit % and Operating Expenses vary.

Your best business would be B. Gross Profit % was 30.0% and Operating Expenses were $3075.63 resulting in a Net Income of $5924.37.

Notice how Net Income differs when Gross Profit % and Operating Expenses differ.

The goal of a business is to maximize sales with a projected Gross Profit %, that remains the same or increases, and to keep Operating Expenses the same or less.

That is the reason businessmen look at their financial statements each month. When actual results differ from projections, the business owner attempts to find out why.

.

NET INCOME DIFFERENT DUE TO DIFFERENCES IN GROSS PROFIT % AND OPERATING EXPENSES

What if sales were $30,000.00 in each business?

	Business A		Business B		Business C	
A)Sales						
	$30,000.00	100.0%	**$30,000.00**	100.0%	**$30,000.00**	100.0%
B) Cost of Goods Sold						
	$24,000.00	**80.0%**	$21,000.00	**70.0%**	$24,000.00	**80.0%**
A-B=C						
C) Gross Profit						
	$ 6,000.00	**20.0%**	$ 9,000.00	**30.0%**	$ 6,000.00	**20.0%**
D) Operating Expense						
	$ 3,075.63	**10.3%**	$ 3,075.63	**10.3%**	$ 5,075.63	**16.9%**
C=D=E						
E) Net Income						
	$ 2,924.37	**9.7%**	$ 5,924.37	**19.7%**	$ 924.37	**3.1%**

PROJECTED

Vs.

ACTUAL

INCOME STATEMENT

Sales projections are very important is computing the monthly projected Net Income.

The Gross Profit % and Operating Expenses should be projected and monitored monthly.

Then each month, you can determine whether you met your projected numbers. If not, good management will try to determine why.

Information refers to next page:

PROJECTED vs ACTUAL INCOME STATEMENT

Note that the actual cost of apples was $13,500.00 or 94.7%. The projected Gross Profit % was 25.0%.

In this case, management would do their best to find the reason for the low Gross Profit %. That projected Net Income of $2,450.00 resulted in an actual loss of $1,130.00.

Some reasons for extra cost:

> **Cashier not ringing up sales**
> **Sales Invoices not recorded**
> **Customer or employees stealing inventory**
> **Outside vendor not delivering purchased amount of product or services**
> **Fraud payments to non-existing vendors**

Your accounting system should be set up as if everyone is a potential thief, because you would not hire someone whom you did not trust.

INCOME STATEMENT

PROJECTED VS. ACTUAL

Apples sold in January

	Projected		Actual	
A) Sale of Apples:	$16,000.00	100.0%	$14,250.00	100.0%
B) Cost of Apples	$12,000.00	75.0%	$13,500.00	94.7%
C) Gross Profit	$ 4,000.00	25.0%	$ 750.00	5.3%

Operating Expenses

	Projected		Actual	
Rent	$ 1,000.00		$ 1,000.00	
Labor (salary)	500.00		800.00	
Payroll Taxes	50.00		80.00	
D) Total Op. Expenses	$ 1550.00	9.7%	$ 1,880.00	13.2%

C-D=E

E) Net Income	$ 2,450.00	15.3%	$(1,130.00)	(7.9%)

This is what business management is all about—finding out why Gross Profit % and Net Income are less than projected.

Wrong calculation – GROSS PROFIT %

Easy to make this mistake

Wrong calculation – GROSS PROFIT %

Businessman thinks that to get a 25% gross profit, he should multiply the cost by 125%. See why this is wrong.

Note that the cost of $12,000.00 was multiplied by 125% to get a 25% gross profit %. However, the example shows only a 20% markup.

Multiply: $12,000.00 x 125% = $15,000.00.

A) Apple Sales	$15,000.00	100.0%
B) Cost of Apples	$12,000.00	80.0%
C) Gross Profit	$ 3,000.00	20.0%

The correct calculation:

100.0% minus 25% desired Gross Profit = 75%

Divide the $12,000 Cost of Apples by .75 = $16,000.00

Proof:

Apple Sales--------$ 16,000.00 100.0%

Cost of Apples---- $12,000.00   75.0%

Gross Profit------- $ 4,000.00   25.0%

COMMENTARY

GROSS PROFIT %

GROSS PROFIT % in RETAIL, SERVICE, SERVICE AND PARTS, AND MANUFACTURING

This book emphasizes the importance of the Gross Profit %. **The Gross Profit % is the Gross Profit amount divided by the Sales or Income amount on the Income Statement. (see p.28)** As mentioned, this percent is a very important management number. If it does not meet projections, you can look at the sales, purchases and inventory amounts to determine what is causing the lower than projected Gross Profit. The reason that many startup businesses fail is that they never have an accurate Gross Profit % which is used to manage. They may have financial problems before they realize that the Gross Profit % number needs to be managed.

The **Service** and **Service and Parts businesses** can be like retail where the Gross Profit % needs to be continually managed. Or it can be like a service business where the sales amount and profit on each bid job can be greatly different. Hence in those situations, the owner often looks at the Net Profit. If that does not meet his projections, he will look at his bidding process as well as the other factors affecting profit.

Manufacturing can be like the retail business in watching Gross Profit % or it can be like the service business where there are bid jobs, the sales amount and profit on each job varying greatly.

THEFT can affect INCOME as well as COST OF GOODS SOLD:

Are you aware of the many ways that a business can be subject to theft?

Preventing theft can increase net profit. If the cashier does not ring up the sale and puts the money in his/her pocket, you have less profit. This is particularly true for small companies. If the cashier does not give a receipt to a cash paying customer, the sale is not registered in the total sales for that day and the cash-ier can keep the money without checkup detection. I noticed that a Walgreen's store gave the customer $5.00 if the customer was not given a receipt. That was to prevent cashier theft. Many stores have a camera focused on the cash register to deter theft.

Inventory **((A-4) page 60, see pages 65-66 for more details)** can be stolen. It is important that every purchase is accounted for before you sign the vendor's receipt ticket. As mentioned above: cameras can detect employee or vendor theft. One of my gro-cery clients signed a ticket that a certain number of loaves of bread had been delivered. But he caught the bread delivery man covering up some of the loaves and trying to take them back to his truck. He probably wanted to re-sell that bread to another grocer for cash.

Each person who handles cash has to be responsible for that cash each day. I set up a control system for a business that han-dled lots of cash. The day I set the system up, $1,000.00 was missing. Two people had been handling the cash; the owner could not legally say who stole it.
Remember that only a seemingly honest person can steal from you. You would never hire a person to handle cash who seemed to be dishonest.

SALES ARE AFFECTED BY THEFT:

1) Cashier not ringing up sales:

As mentioned above, if the cashier does not ring up the sale, the cash will still balance at the end of the day. The cashier does not offset money for that sale, since the sale was not recorded. But the store loses the profit on the sale as well as the cost of the inventory.

Example:

The register tape shows sales for the day of $542.00--that is the amount of sales actually recorded. If $15.00 of sales were not rung up, the cash register tape would not show the omission. If the cashier accounts for the $542.00, the cash would still be balanced. The $15.00 could be in the cashier's pocket or he/she could have let a friend walk out with unpaid items not recorded.

2) Invoices not recorded:

A company stockholder did not record all customer invoices. The other stockholders realized the numbers were not sensible. I tried unsuccessfully to get copies of the voided invoices to enter into the books (accounting records). I gave the accounting records back to the company, since I had not found the reason the company's profit was smaller than expected. About a year later, I learned the unbelievable. The 3rd stockholder, who prepared the invoices and deposited the money, was an embezzler. The amount of the missing invoices was kept by the 3rd stockholder.

I learned an important lesson. Usually the individual who can successfully embezzle is the individual who seems honest. From my observation, it never entered my mind that he was capable of embezzling money. If the same situation happened today, I would e-mail all the accounting records to the other 2 individuals so that they could examine the books for any dishonesty.

Also I would recommend that all work be logged in at the beginning of the job and end of the job, by two different individuals, and to check to determine that the job was billed.

Make sure that you have controls in place, so that all sales and all invoices are entered into your accounting record.

OTHER SOLUTIONS
TO PREVENT THEFT BY CASHIER:

Do you need other solutions to prevent theft?

1) **A specialized camera system** can be put into the store. Then if any criminal activity is suspected, the pictures can be viewed.

2) **A shopping service** can be hired. The shopping service will send customers to buy. The checker is watched to determine if all transactions are recorded.

3) Employees can be carefully screened with **background checks** and their references checked. However due to potential lawsuits, a previous employer may not divulge damaging information.

4) **Adding Machines** should not be available to the checker or cashier for use at the cash register. The cashier can give an adding machine tape as receipt for the purchase and not ring the sale up on the register.

5) **Daily Cash Checkup Sheet** is a daily reconciliation of cash. It is used mainly for retail businesses. If this cash checkup sheet is not used, employees will often steal your profits and you won't even know it. See example: **pages 147 – 153.**

FAST TRACK

BALANCE SHEET

LEARNING

Assets: What you own

Liabilities: What you owe

Capital: What you own minus what you owe

Example: You own $100,000.00

            You owe $ 40,000.00

            Your Capital $ 60,000.00

Information below refers to next page:

INDIVIDUAL BALANCE SHEET

This is an individual Balance Sheet similar in format to the business Balance Sheet.

Assets are everything the individual owns totaling $300,000.00 in this example.

Liabilities are the amount of all the individual owes totaling $162,000.00 in this example.

Capital (Net Worth for an individual) is the difference between $300,000.00 minus $162,000.00 = $138,000.00

Assets - Liabilities = Capital

So if you sold all your assets for $300,000.00 and paid your liabilities of $162,000.00, you would have $138,000.00 cash.

All assets on the individual Balance Sheet are usually shown at market value. The business Balance Sheet shows fixed assets at cost.

INDIVIDUAL BALANCE SHEET

Comparison to your assets:

ASSETS:

Cash	$ 15,000.00
Savings	15,000.00
Retirement Accounts	20,000.00
Residence	225.000.00
Vehicles	20,000.00
Coin Collection	5,000.00
A) TOTAL ASSETS:	**$300,000.00** (a)

LIABILITIES:

Credit Cards Payable	$ 7,000.00
Mortgage Payable	155,000.00
B) TOTAL LIABILITIES:	**$162,000.00** (b)

C) CAPITAL	**$138,000.00** (c)

D) TOTAL LIABILITIES & CAPITAL $300,000.00
Total liabilities (b) + capital (c) = total assets (a)

Assets (a) - Total Liabilities (b) = Capital (c)
$300,000.00 - $162,000.00 = $138,000.00

See page 60-61   Balance Sheet

ANALYZING THE BALANCE SHEET:

THE BALANCE SHEET IS DIVIDED INTO 3 PARTS:

1) ASSETS (A-1 – A-17):   **What you own**
                                                            $27,342.12

2) LIABILITIES (B-1 – B-6):   **What you owe**
                                                            ($ 8,375.01)

3) CAPITAL (C-1 – C-4): **What you have left over when you pay all Liabilities**   **$18,967.11**

Proof:
Assets: $27,342.12

minus
Liabilities: 8,375.01

equals
Capital: $18,967.11

See page 60-61   Balance Sheet

WHAT YOU THINK IT IS:

The balance sheet is an equation: Assets ($27,342.12) - Liabilities ($8,375.01) = Capital ($18,967.11). See previous page.

Hence, you would think that if you could convert all your assets to cash and pay your liabilities, you would have the cash shown in the Capital Section.

However on a business Balance Sheet, that is usually not true.

THE BALANCE SHEET CAN BE A MISLEADING STATEMENT   (See next page)

Basically all assets except for inventory and securities are valued at cost. The land you bought for your business location cost $1,000.00 and is now worth $1,000,000.00, but is still recorded as $1,000.00 on the books. Note however, small businesses seldom buy land through the C Corporation (pages 161-164), since the corporation would pay tax on the profits of the sale of the land and the owner of the corporation would pay tax on any money distributed as a dividend—double taxation.

Fixed assets such as furniture & fixtures (A-10), equipment (A-12) and vehicles (A-14) are recorded at cost and adjusted by Allowance for Depreciation in a separate account. You can't tell the value of fixed assets by looking at the Balance Sheet.
Accounts Receivable (A-3) may be overstated if some Accounts Receivable amounts are uncollectible.
Inventory (A-4) may be over or understated depending upon the diligence given to having an accurate account.
Accounts Payable (B-1) This figure may be incorrect.

A BUSINESS BALANCE SHEET

BALANCE SHEET

A ASSETS: March 31, 20___

A-1	Cash-in-Bank		$ 3,432.11
A-2	Cash-on-Hand		200.00
A-3	Accounts Receivable		650.00
A-4	Inventory		2,000.00
A-5	Prepaid Insurance		600.00
A-6	Prepaid Interest		825.00
A-7	Return Check		20.00
A-8	Due from Employee		40.00
A-9	Total Current Assets		$ 7,767.11
A-10	Furniture and Fixture	$ 1,625.01	
A-11	(-) Allowance for Depreciation	10.00	$1,615.01
A-12	Equipment	$11,760.00	
A-13	(-) Allowance for Depreciation	280.00	11,480.00
A-14	Trucks	$ 6,000.00	
A-15	(-) Allowance for Depreciation	300.00	5,700.00
A-16	**Improvements**	**$ 600.00**	
A-17	**(-) Allowance for Depreciation**	**20.00**	**580.00**
A-18	Deposits		200.00
A-19	**TOTAL ASSETS**		**$27,342.12**

B   LIABILITIES:

B-1   Accounts Payable $ 560.00

B-2	Withholding & FICA Texas Payable	200.00
B-3	Sales Taxes Payable	240.00
B-4	Accrued Payroll Payable	200.00
B-5	**Insurance Payable**	**600.00**
B-6	Notes Payable	6,575.01
B-7	**TOTAL LIABILITIES**	**$ 8,375.01**

C   CAPITAL:

C-1	Capital, Store Owner*	$24,000.00
C-2	Withdrawal, Store Owner	3,957.26
C-3	Current Earnings, Store Owner (Loss	(1,075.63)
C-4	**TOTAL CAPITAL**	**$18,967.11**
D	**TOTAL LIABILITIES & CAPITAL**	**$27,342.12**

$27,342.12 Assets = $8,375.01 Liabilities & $18,967.11 Capital

> *C-1 Individual and Partnership
> *C-1 Corporation capital account is Common Stock
> The Business Balance Sheet shown above and the Individual Balance Sheet shown previously are both divided into 3 sections.

Each item on the Balance Sheet is discussed in detail on **pages 62-73**.

BALANCE SHEET DETAIL

Each account shown on the Balance Sheet **(pages 60-61)** is explained in detail on the following pages.

THE BALANCE SHEET DETAIL
A) ASSETS

A-1 CASH

The cash account balance should equal the bank reconciliation amount which is your check register balance (you enter all deposits and checks and other transactions that effect your bank account balance). When **reconciling your bank account**, add to your check register any items you do not have there that are shown on your bank statement. The bank reconciliation proves that your check register agrees with your bank statement.

Example:

The bank reconciliation equals:

Bank Balance on Bank Statement   3/31/17--- $15,034.65

        Add: **Deposits in-transit**--deposits, usually on last day of month, that post on next month's bank statement.

                        3/31/17 $ 2,000.00
                  Total------------ $17,034.65

        MINUS: **Total of outstanding checks**
        3/25/14 – ck#45-------- 450.25
        3/30/14—ck#46------- 200.00
        3/31/14---ck#47---- 12,952.29   13,602.54
Reconciled Bank Reconciliation   3/31/17   **$ 3,432.11**

The amount of $3,432.11 shown above should equal the check register amount.

After you have completed the reconciliation, check any deposits-in-transit (shown above as $2,000.00).

Unless they are at the end of the month, find out why the old deposits did not post to the bank account.

It is important to reconcile your bank statement every month. If a bank error is over 30 days old, the bank may not reimburse you for any bank error.

A-2 CASH-ON-HAND
This account is normally for retail businesses such as grocery stores, etc. that need to give change to their customers.

A-3   ACCOUNTS RECEIVABLES
These are the amounts you have billed your customers for products you have sold or services you have performed. Every customer payment on their Accounts Receivable balances reduces the total owed to your company.

The Accounts Receivables amount shown on the balance sheet may be overstated when some of the receivables are uncollectible or not billed correctly.

An aging Accounts Receivable schedule showing past due invoices in 0-30, 31-60, 61-90 and over 90 days categories could be analyzed for collection problems. Any amount over 30 days late should be checked to see if it is really owed; if so, that customer may be contacted.

Note that an **uncollectible Accounts Receivable** is charged to an expense account--**Bad Debts (D-3 on Income Statement)** which reduces net income. Failure to expense uncollectable Accounts Receivables to Bad Debts **(D-3)** results in the net income being overstated. This area, in addition to Inventory, is where the resulting profits can be overstated.

A-4 INVENTORY

Inventory is the merchandise you have on hand that you are go-ing to sell. Inventory theft can occur in many ways dependent upon your type of business. If you do not compare the amount of merchandise received to the purchase invoice at the time of the delivery, you leave your business open to theft. Theft of in-ventory reduces income.

If your inventory is calculated by the computer based on pur-chases and sales, you could get that computer printout at the end of the month and make an adjustment to the inventory fig-ure to arrive at your real net income. If the inventory items are not on the computer, you can just count the items and price at cost each item.

Example:
      You have a computer printout that shows 508 different items, the number of items being grouped into their respective categories.

508 items separated into 3 categories:

Category	# of items	Cost per item	Total
A	178	$5.00	$890.00
B	300	$3.00	$900.00
C	30	$7.00	$210.00
			$2000.00

A manual inventory is a count of every item multiplied by the cost of each item. Any difference between the manual count value and Inventory amount shown on the Balance Sheet is rec-orded as an adjustment to Inventory, reducing or increasing in-come.

It is very disheartening when a business owner thought the prof-its were meeting projections during the year, only to find out at the end of the year, that the **decrease in inventory erased the year's profit shown to date.**

If the businessman had taken inventory during the year and noticed that his profits were lower than projected, a management adjustment such as increasing sales prices, cutting costs, looking for various kinds of theft, etc. could have been made. Making such changes may have increased income.

INVENTORY is the one area where income can be unethically substantially increased, with no basis for the increase, by making a journal entry to adjust to a higher inventory.

If a profit increase is the result of an inventory increase in a period of no sales increase, you may want to ask the question, "Why is the inventory more?" There may be a legitimate answer such as an increase in purchases due to a "good deal".
If your business has inventory, always find out how the inventory was computed and periodically check some items on the list that make up the total inventory. As mentioned before, net income may be overstated due to overstated inventory.

A-5 – A-8 OTHER CURRENT ASSETS:
The following are 4 current assets:

A-5 Prepaid Insurance- normally the amount of insurance paid for several months up to a year or by monthly payments. The calculation for the expense portion is shown on pages **16-17 (D-12 on Income Statement).**

Brief example (continued top of next page):
$600.00 for a 6 month policy paid on 3/31/17=$100.00 per month insurance expense.

Balance Sheet   3/31/17
Prepaid Insurance $600.00

Balance Sheet   4/30/17
Prepaid Insurance $500.00
($600.00 minus $100.00 monthly expense)

Balance Sheet   5/31/17
Prepaid Insurance $400.00
($600.00 minus $200.00 monthly expenses to date)

A-6 Prepaid Interest- normally the amount of interest paid for several months to usually a year(s) into the future by a note. It would be calculated the same as insurance above.

A-7 Return Check-the customer's check that you deposit in your bank that was returned to you by your bank because of insufficient funds in the customer's account, account closed, etc. By reading the date of these checks, you can better determine whether the return check accounts should be reduced by the amount of the checks and expensed to Bad Debt **(D-3 on Income Statement)**. (expensed = recorded as an expense)

A-8 Due from Employees--is the amount loaned to your employees that has not been paid back.

By determining that the employees, who owe money to the company, are currently employed and have made recent payments, you can better determine whether the Due from Employee account should be reduced and the amount recorded as expensed to Bad Debt **(D-3 on Income Statement)**.

A-10, A-12, A-14   FIXED ASSETS:
Assets such as equipment, fixtures, vehicles, building and land are recorded at cost. These cost amounts stay the same

throughout the holding of these assets, even though the value of these assets usually goes down (except for land and maybe buildings). A fixed percent of the assets (except for land) is recorded as Depreciation Expense on the Income Statement **(See page 11, D-7 & page 15)** and Allowance for Depreciation **(A-11, A-13, A-15)** on the Balance Sheet. This is a bookkeeping entry and does not involve the cash account. (Congress can change the rules concerning Depreciation at any time.)

A-11, A-13, A-15 ALLOWANCE FOR DEPRECIATION:
Allowance for Depreciation is the depreciation calculated from the date of the asset purchase to the date the financial statements are issued. *("depreciation"* **explained D-7, page 15)**

Book Depreciation is normally deprecation over a set period of years until fully depreciated. This is usually the amount shown on the income statement each year.

The Depreciation Schedule shows the date of purchase, item purchased, the amount of purchase, the depreciation taken to date, and depreciation for the current year, etc.

Analyze the Depreciation Schedule and determine whether the company has in its possession the items shown. If you want the value of all the fixed assets, appraise each item.

Note that there is also a Depreciation Schedule for *tax depreciation* which normally shows more deprecation in the first year the assets are purchased. Increased depreciation results in lower net income and usually lower income tax in the first year(s).

B) LIABILITIES

B-1 ACCOUNTS PAYABLE
This is the amount owed to your suppliers or vendors. The **Accounts Payable Aging Schedule** shows the purchase invoices still unpaid and is often listed in categories of 0-30, 31-60, 61-90, over 90 days late. The amount of Accounts Payable can be deliberately understated to show less expense and hence more profit.

Any past due Accounts Payable invoices could adversely affect your credit. Different companies have different policies. If you are past the payment deadline, your vendor could make you pay the total amount for future purchases on delivery (COD). Check all past due invoices.

B-2 – B-4 CURRENT LIABILITES

B-2 Withholding & FICA Taxes Payable (Social Security taxes & Medicare taxes)--the amount owed for payroll taxes:
Social Security taxes are a combination of the amount of Withholding plus 2 x the FICA taxes deducted from the employee's check.

There are big penalties when a payment is not made within the time limit. At the end of each year, the Internal Revenue Service will notify you of your time limit to make payroll tax deposits for the next year based on your annual payroll through September. Check the date the required tax deposit has to be made. If your Federal payroll tax liability is at least $50,000.00 for the prior IRS year, the rule now requires you to make the tax deposits within a few days of payroll depending on what day of the week the current payroll checks are dated. These rules can change.

Anyone, employee, business owner, or officer responsible for paying these payroll taxes to the Internal Revenue Service **may be held personally liable** when the payroll taxes are not paid by the company.

B-3 Sales Taxes Payable- the amount owed for the local and state sales taxes collected or use taxes.

It is very important for you to know the rules pertaining to your business and your industry. The tax amount owed can be substantial over a 4 year audit period or for whatever period your state laws authorize a possible sales tax audit.

Also, it is very important that you are up to date filing your reports and paying the sales tax; otherwise the government could freeze your bank account. Depending on your state laws, that can happen quickly.

B-4 Accrued Salary Payable- the amount owed for unpaid salary on the last day of the month.

Example:
>Check #1234 paid to Joe Smith dated 3/31/17 for work thru 3/29/17.
>Owed Smith $200.00 for **end of month work done 3/30/17 & 3/31/17 but paid on April 13.**
>The accrued salary payable is $200.00 (not paid in March but paid on April 13).

It is important to show a correct Accrued Salary Payable at the end of the month, so your labor cost is correct for that month and so you can have a management oriented financial statement.

B-5 Accounts Payable-Insurance is the monthly amount that you will pay for insurance premiums over a period of time.

Example	Total
Yearly insurance-------------------	$600.00
Minus: Down-payments	0.00
Payable-Other	$600.00
(Pay $100.00 a month for 6 months.)	

All insurance payments are recorded to this account when the Accounts Payable-Insurance is set up. The total amount of $600.00 is Prepaid Insurance and is amortized monthly and recorded as expensed on the Income Statement as shown on **(D-12, page 11)**.

B-6 Notes Payable- the original amount of the loan minus any principal payments you have made.

The note does not include the interest. Each note payment is broken down into the amount that reduces the Notes Payable and the amount recorded as interest expense. If $500.00 is paid, $400.00 is applied to the principal (If that is the computed amount and reduces the Notes Payable while in this case $100.00 is paid for interest and is shown on the Income Statement as interest expense **(D-13, page 11)**.

C) CAPITAL

C-1 Capital, Store Owner-
This is the term used for the **individual business** that is not incorporated and for partners in a partnership.

Corporation: This capital account is classified as Common Stock.

C-2 Withdrawal, Store Owner-
This is the amount of a payment, etc. to the owner of an unincorporated business or the partner of a partnership that is a personal withdrawal.

All payments to the corporation owners are either recorded as salary, dividend distributions, or advances that have to be repaid.

Sub-S Corporation- payments to the corporate owners are salary, or a charge to the withdrawal account titled Accumulated Adjustment Account or advances that have to be paid back.

Retained Earnings- the accumulated earnings from the beginning of the business minus any dividends and other adjustments.

C-3 Current Earnings- the earnings since the beginning of the year to the present date. At the end of the year the amount is added to Capital (for sole proprietorship and partners of partnerships) and to Retained Earnings (for corporations).

Generally, Capital is the money invested into the business, plus business earnings, minus any withdrawals, business losses, and other miscellaneous adjustments.

Other items not previously discussed:

A. OTHER ASSETS:

A-18 Deposits—normally money paid and held as security for payment of utilities, etc.

Not Included on Balance Sheet, page 60.

Prepaid Rent--normally rent for the last month of a lease

Goodwill--the amount paid by the buyer of a business that is more than the cost of the inventory, fixed assets, etc.
   Example:
   You paid $500,000.00 for a business:
   That included the following cost breakdown:

Accounts Receivables------- -------	$105,230.00
Inventory---------------------------	185,000.00
Fixed Assets------------------------	75,000.00
Total -----------------------------	$365,230.00

   Goodwill is $134,770.00 ($500,000.00 minus $365,230.00)

   This $134,770.00 is then amortized yearly like Depreciation (a certain % is shown as expense on the Income Statement each month).

Franchise Costs – the cost of buying a franchise

Securities – Investments: Stocks, bonds, etc.

Improvements – not fixed assets but improvements to property

73

RELATIONSHIP BETWEEN BALANCE SHEET ACCOUNTS

Relationship between Assets and Liabilities accounts can indicate the financial strength of the business.

Information below refers to next page:

Relationship between Balance Sheet Accounts

Cash vs Accounts Payable

If you have $1,000.00 cash but owe $100,000.00, your business has a very good chance of closing.

If you did not have an up-to-date balance sheet, you might not have this information.

A) Assets - B) Liabilities = C) Capital

A) $1,000.00 - **B)** $100,000.00 = **C)** $(99,000.00)

What this statement indicates is that the businessman financed his losses by not paying his payables:

Cash vs. Accounts Payable

Balance Sheet

ASSETS:

Cash $ 1,000.00

A) TOTAL ASSETS $ **1,000.00**

LIABILIIES:
Accounts Payable $100,000.00

B) TOTAL LAIBILITIES   **$100,000.00**

CAPITAL:
Capital $(104,000.00) loss
Current Income   5,000.00
C) TOTAL CAPITAL   **$(99,000.00) loss**

D) TOTAL LIABILITIES & CAPITAL   **$1,000.00**

Information below refers to next page:

Cash & Accounts Receivable vs Accounts Payable

If your balance sheet showed the information on the following page, what would you do?

1) You would probably do your best to collect the Accounts Receivables. Accounts Receivable is the money owed to you for work (services) done or products sold minus payments already received on that account.

2) You would want to find out when the individual payable amounts need to be paid.

3) Then you would match the collection goals with the due dates of the individual payable invoices. Hopefully, the payments of your Accounts Receivables would be available to pay your bills as they become due.

Without this balance sheet, the owner might not have realized the dire situation and the urgency for action.

Cash and Accounts Receivable vs Accounts Payable

Balance Sheet

ASSETS

Cash	$ 1.000.00
Accounts Receivable	100,000.00
A) Total Assets	**$101,000.00**

LIABILITIES

Accounts Payable	$100,000.00
B) Total liabilities	$100,000.00

CAPITAL

CAPITAL	$(4,000.00)
Net Income to date this year	5,000.00
C) Total Capital	$ 1,000.00

D) TOTAL LAIBILITIES & CAPITAL	**$101,000.00**

Assets - Liabilities = Capital

$101,000.00 - $100,000.00 = $1,000.00

Information below refers to next page:

Cash, Accounts Receivable, Inventory
vs Accounts Payable

From the information on this Balance Sheet, management knows there is inventory worth $50,000.00. That inventory can be sold to help pay the payables.

In order to stay in business, management may decide to sell the inventory as soon as possible. Then determine when the accounts payables are due. Collect the receivables and sell the inventory to meet your payment deadlines.

Without this balance sheet, management might not have realized the urgency of the situation.

Cash, Accounts Receivable, Inventory vs Accounts Payable

ASSETS

Cash	$ 1,000.00
Accounts Receivable	100,000.00
Inventory	50,000.00
A) Total Assets	**$151,000.00**

LIABILITIES

Accounts Payable	$100,000.00
B) Total Liabilities	$100,000.00

CAPITAL	$ 46,000.00
Net Income year to date	5,000.00
C) Total Capital	$ 51,000.00

D) TOTAL LIABILITIES & CAPITAL $151,000.00

Assets - Liabilities = Capital

$151,000.00 - $100,000.00 = $51,000.00

RATIOS

Shows the relationship between numbers on the Balance
If you have $10,000.00 cash but owe $1,000.00 that is an
excellent ratio **(10 to 1)**

If you have $1,000.00 cash and owe $10,000.00, that is not a
good ratio **(1 to 10)**

Ratios give a view of the financial strength of the business.

RATIOS:

Ratios show the relationship between numbers on the financial statements. These ratios can be compared to your previous ratios and to industry averages.

Below are examples showing the 2 ratios that indicate if the company is able to pay its bills on time.

Financial Ratios give you an idea of how your business is doing. There are many different ratios. Only 2 ratios are discussed here.

1) Current Ratio: Shows whether you have enough current assets to pay your current liabilities. As mentioned before, Accounts Receivable balances may contain uncollectible amounts and the Inventory balance may be incorrect. The ratio is a guide as to whether or not the company can pay its debts, but you have to look at the underlying assets such as Accounts Receivable and Inventory.

Current Assets/Current Liabilities
$6282.11 /$1,800.00= **3.5**   **Normally 2 to 3 is considered adequate**

Current Assets:
Cash-in-Bank------------- $3,432.11
Cash-on-Hand------------   200.00
Accounts Receivables----   650.00
Inventory------------------   2,000.00
Total----------------------- $6,282.11

Current Liabilities
Accounts Payable $1,800.00

2) Quick or Acid Test ratio: Shows the cash or cash equivalents that you have to pay current liabilities; but not Inventory.

Liquid Assets/Accounts Payable:
$4,282.11/$1800.00 = **2.4**

Cash-in-Bank------------------- $ 3,432.11
Cash-on-Hand----------------   200.00
Accounts Receivable-Current-   650.00
Total Liquid Assets------- $ 4,282.11

Current Liabilities:
Accounts Payable $1,800.00

These two ratios show that the company can easily pay its current debts. If the ratio was less than 1, there may be doubt as to whether the company can pay its debts on time.

ACCRUAL METHOD

VS

CASH ACCOUNTING METHOD

It is very important to use the Accrual Accounting Method for management information.

The Accrual Accounting Method records income when earned and expenses when incurred.

The Cash Accounting Method only records Income as the earned income is received and when the expenses are paid.

Payroll usually has an extra pay period every three months. By accruing the payroll every month, the extra weekly labor costs is distributed over three months. This results in **correct monthly labor costs**.

Always verify your Accounts Receivable and Accounts Payable balance and other payables on the Balance Sheet. If they are incorrect, your Income Statement will be incorrect.

Information below refers to next page:

ACCRUAL VS. CASH ACCOUNTING METHODS
VERY IMPORTANT – VERY IMPORTANT
FOR MANAGING

Accrual numbers show the actual amount billed to your customers. The **Cash Method** shows how much of your billing you actually collected.

Note that using the Accrual Method in the example:
        Sales income for March was $10,000.00.

Note that under the Cash Method:
        Sales income for March was $14,000.00.

The Cash Method shows $4,000.00 more income than the Accrual Method. (14,000.00 less 10,000.00)

You can't be an effective manager using cash based financial statements. Using the Accrual Method, you would still have the option to file your tax return on the cash basis when you meet the IRS guidelines under IRS rules today.

It is never wise to make decisions based on a Cash Method financial statement because the income is based on collections rather than on sales.

Accrual Method (Actual Sales Numbers and Expense numbers):

Accrual Method - The sales actually billed
Sales for January---------------$ 5,000.00
Sales for February-------------$ 8,000.00
Sales for March---------------$10,000.00

Cash Method (Income received and Expenses paid):

Cash Method - Sales for this or prior months paid

In the above example of billing for the months of January, February, March, the following **amount** was **collected in March**:

From January Sales-----------$ 2,000.00 of the $5,000.00 (above)
From February Sales----------- 6,000.00 of the $8,000.00 (above)
From March Sales-------------- 6,000.00 of the $10, 00.00 (above)
Total March Collections-----$14,000.00

Information below refers to next page:

Accrual vs. Cash Accounting Method

Note that Accrual Method shows actual sales (income) of product sales or services you have provided for the month or any other period such as a year or three month. The Cash Method shows what billing invoices you have collected.

The Accrual Method also shows the actual costs for any month or any other period. The Cash Method shows actual payments.

Note that receipts on the Cash Method were $1,000.00 more than on the accrual basis.

The purchases were $3,000.00 less using the Cash Method rather than the Accrual Method.

That resulted in $4,000.00 more gross profit using the Cash Method.

The Gross Profit, using the Cash Method, could have been less had the Cash Method had less receipts and more expenses.

Cash Method misleading for management: **WARNING**

Unknowingly, many **members of an organization or business** do not realize that their approved Cash Method statements has resulted in a misleading Income Statement & Balance Sheet.

Members can be fooled about the financial condition of an organization or company using the Cash Accounting Method.

ACCRUAL VS CASH METHOD

	6-1-2017 to
Accrual Method	6-30-2017

A) Apple sales whether or not paid-----	$ 6,500.00	100.0%
Minus:		
B) Total purchases whether or not paid--	$ 4,000.00	61.5%
C) Gross Profit---------------------------------	$ 2,500.00	38.5%

	6-1-2017 to
Cash Method*	6-30-2017

A) Apple sales that were paid---------------	$7,500.00	100.0%
Minus:		
B) Purchases (bills) that were paid--------	$1,000.00	13.3%
C) Gross Profit-----------------------------	$ 6,500.00	86.7%

*assumes same inventory for both Cash & Accrual Method

How can you manage your business with the Cash Method acounting when you can't rely on an accurate Gross Profit %?

VERIFY

INCOME STATEMENT
&
BALANCE SHEET

AT THE END OF THE MONTH

By understanding the items on the Income Statement and Balance Sheet, you will be able to make the check list to verify that the Balance Sheet number agrees with the detail.

Then you can go through the General Ledger of all the accounts and determine whether the individual items are correct.

If you don't know what an entry is for, ask. It could be fraud. Verifying the numbers can help prevent fraud.

When you go through this verification process for several months, the time involved should become much less.

Determine that on the **Balance Sheet** all the money owed you is shown as **Receivables** and all Payables are shown as **payables.** Otherwise, your Income Statement could be incorrect since those receivables and payables affect the accrual Income Statement.

1) Have your accountant give you the **Bank Statement** & **Bank Reconciliation** for the end of the month.

Look quickly at each check in the bank statement. **Ask: "Did I sign each check and am I familiar with the name on the check?" Compare the name on each check with the name shown in the General Ledger Cash Account.**

Several years ago, a client's employee stole the company bank checks, filled them out , and used them. I caught this when I reconciled the bank statement. If your accountant is entering unauthorized checks into the accounting records and reconciling the bank statement you may miss this theft, unless you check the records yourself each month.

2) Have your accountant give you an **Aging Schedule of Accounts Receivables.**
It should show you by the 0-30, 31-60, 61-90 and over 90 day classification of past-due invoices what your customers owe. Check the over 30, 60, and 90 days categories—why haven't they paid? Find out why.

3) Have your accountant give you an **Aging Schedule of Accounts Payables.**
Determine why all over 30 days payables have not been paid.

4) Get an inventory detail of your **Merchandise** (retail business), **Manufacture Inventory** or **Job Costs** (service or service/parts) at the end of the month that have not been sold or billed—this is especially important when you start a business. As was mentioned before, the accountant could increase your inventory with just a Journal Entry to show an increase in profit. This could be a temptation for the office manager in a business that has more than one owner. Showing sufficient profits allows the office manager to impress the other owners that he is the right manager. If the inventory was estimated, you need to know on what basis it was estimated.

5) **Make sure all the above report balances agree with the equivalent amount on the Balance Sheet**.

6) Have your accountant give you the **General Ledger** of **all your accounts.**

    a)   The General Ledger shows the activity of every account on the Income Statement and Balance Sheet. Activity means checks, deposits, and adjusting entries. **Check every General Ledger entry of the Assets accounts.** Doing this every month will give you a good feel for those accounts. After a few months of checking the entries, you will be able to quickly glance through them.

       Note: The **Assets** section (prepaid expenses, etc.) of the Balance Sheet is <u>where expenses are often hidden as assets</u> when someone wants the business to show more profits.

    b) **Check the General Ledger Liability accounts:**

       Payroll Taxes & Sales Taxes--check when the balances shown on the Balance Sheet are due. If they are past due, you will probably be charged a penalty. Check any other liability such as accrued payroll (money earned for days worked this month but not paid until the next month). Also check any Notes Payable balances (monthly payments made to creditors) by calling the bank or checking records.

    c) **Check the General Ledger Income Account:**

       If your business is retail, you probably used the daily checkup sheet to record your sales **(see pages 147-153)**.

       If your business is Service, Service/Parts, or Manufacturing, you probably billed your customer. In either case, compare the General Ledger Income Account entries with the pertinent sales invoices, etc.

d) **Check the General Ledger Cost of Sales or Cost of Operations and Expenses.**

Determine whether all the General Ledger Cost of Sales or Cost of Operations and Expenses listed are in the correct accounts. If you are not familiar with an item, get a copy of the purchase invoice. You may uncover embezzlement. If your Balance Sheet is right every month, your Income Statement will be correct.

Note that the net income on the Balance Sheet **(C-3 Current Earnings)** in the Capital Section is the same as the year-to-date income amount on the Income Statement **(E)**.

7) If in doubt, ask questions. If not satisfied with the answer, have the accountant give you the source documents such as invoice, deposit slip, check, etc.

Remember, only a seemingly honest person can steal from you. You would not knowingly hire a thief to do your accounting or cashier work.

CASH FLOW

Cash Flow is critical for the survival for a business that has limited cash and access to cash.

Even if you have good profits, having more cash going out than coming in can create financial hardship in the short term when the business does not have necessary cash or access to cash or credit.

Income often does not equal cash, especially when some companies do not pay for 90 days and purchases that are not expenses are incurred.

Information below refers to next page:

PROFIT BUT NO CASH

Did you know that cash on hand does not equal profit?

I will always remember a question that a businessman asked: "How can I show a profit when I do not have money in the bank?" Money in the bank and profit are two different computations.

Note that **the purchase of assets or payments of liabilities are not expenses**.

In this example, the note payment of $800.00 and the $200.00 spent on office furniture are not expenses.

PROFIT BUT NO CASH

EXAMPLE:	PROFIT COMPUTATION	CASH FLOW COMPUTATION
Sales-----------------	$4,000.00	$ 4,000.00
Minus:		
Rent Expense	$3,000.00	$ 3,000.00
Net Profit	**$1,000.00**	**$ 1,000.00**
Minus:		
Note Payment		$ 800.00
Office Furniture		$ 200.00
Total		$ 1,000.00
Net Cash	**$1,000.00**	**$ 0.00**

(Net Profit minus non-expenses = Net Cash)

Assumes funds received for all sales and all disbursements paid for the items above.

Information below refers to next page:

ACCOUNTS RECEIVABLE CASH FLOW

Do you know how accounts receivable affects cash flow?

Accounts Receivable is the total of the different unpaid amounts you have billed your customers for products or ser-vices.

Many people that start a business do not realize that they may not get paid right away. In the example on the next page, the $50,000.00 worth of sales may not be fully paid for 30 to 90 days.

The owner is still responsible for making payroll, paying rent and utilities, paying bills, notes, etc. Often the bigger the company, the slower the payment of your Accounts Receivables billings. That is the reason small cash strapped businesses often do not work for big companies without assurance of getting paid by a certain date.

ACCOUNTS RECEIVABLE CASH FLOW

	Month
Sales	$50,000.00
Accounts Receivable	$50,000.00
Cash	$ 0.00

Even though there was $50,000.00 in sales, no payment for those sales was received. Hence no cash was received to pay your bills.

When you sell products or provide services, don't be bashful about asking when you will be paid (assuming your access to cash is limited).

CASH FLOW

Do you know when you could get into a cash bind?

Many small business start without a Cash Flow Projection and are very successful, but many are not.

The most important point to get right is your Cash Flow Projection. Usually a business will fail if it does not have the cash, or credit, or access to cash to make necessary purchases to continue in operation.

The cash outflow is the cash you pay your vendors or any other entity. When you get behind in paying your bills, your major supplier might not accept partial payment and have you pay COD (pay total amount when you receive their shipment). If their product is necessary for business to continue, the business can fail unless you find another supplier that gives you credit, or unless you are able to obtain cash from another source.

Customer sales in a non-retail business are often made on credit for 30, 60, or 90 days. Often, the bigger the company, the slower they pay.

Though the biggest error in a business plan is overestimating sales, a realistic Cash Flow Projection is critical if you have limited cash or limited access to cash.

To make it easier to figure your cash flow, make a future check register (record for the future rather than for the present). Project all the cash to be received for a period and all the checks to be written for that period. Keep that projection for 1 to 3 months ahead depending on your available cash and credit.

BREAKEVEN POINT

Breakeven refers to the amount of sales needed to show 0 profit.

A projected Gross Profit % and total Operating Expenses allow you to compute the breakeven point.

This gives the owner a ballpark figure of the amount of income needed to breakeven.

Information below refers to next page:

BREAKEVEN POINT

The Breakeven Point is the point at which you make **0** profit with a fixed Gross Profit % and fixed Operating Expenses **(page 11, D-32)**.

Some Operating Expenses are not the same from month to month. In that case, this computation gives you a general idea where the profit breakeven point is.

BREAKEVEN POINT CALCULATION

Example:
Gross profit % = 25% **(page 27 – 33)**
Operating expenses: $1500.00

Divide 1500.00 by .25 = $6000.00 sales needed to break-even or have 0 Net Income.

Proof:
A) Sales------------------ $6,000.00 100.0%

Cost of apples--------- $4,500.00 75.0%
B) Gross Profit------------$1,500.00 25.0%

D) Operating Expenses:
Rent $1000.00
Labor------- 500.00 $1,500.00 25.0%

Net Income   0

LESSONS LEARNED

FROM

7 MANAGEMENT STORIES

MANAGEMENT STORIES:

EFFECT OF TAKING MONTHLY INVENTORY

This man is a pro when it comes to running a business. He usually takes inventory every month to determine his actual costs. **(See page 60, A-4 & pages 65-66 for explanation.)** He looked at his merchandise costs in relation to income to determine whether his merchandise costs were getting out of line.

He had just raised his price when 1973 Federal Wage-Price Controls to control inflation went into effect, meaning he could not increase any prices without the approval of the government. If he had not kept an eye on costs, he would have been stuck with an inflationary product cost not offset by the price increase.

His emphasis on quality and price has made the company very successful.

MANAGING FROM FINANCIAL STATEMENTS—RETAIL BUSINESS

This guy was dissatisfied with his bookkeeper. When I looked at what he had, it was apparent that his bookkeeper was competent. He had the daily check-up sheet to tie in all activity **(See pages 147-153)**. It is almost mandatory at a grocery store and many retail businesses to follow this daily procedure. The problem was that the bookkeeper did not do thorough work. By not having an accurate accrual system **(See pages 87-91)**, his Gross Profit % and his Net Income were continually wrong. **An accurate Gross Profit Percent (pages 27-33) is probably the most important retail management number on the Income**

Statement. When those numbers don't meet projections, a good manager will investigate right away.

This business owner was a great manager, the epitome of a very successful business owner. If any management change was needed, he would review and take action. He used the accurate financial statements to determine what financial decisions had to be made and then put the necessary changes into effect. And he continually strived to determine if anything extra could be done to make his business more profitable. Remember, most businesses should keep the books on the Accrual Basis **(pages 87-89)**. Businessmen who manage like him usually have higher rates of success.

He bought another grocery store business. After operating it for a few years, he sold it to a former Weingarten employee who had many years in the business. The new owner did a fabulous job running this store. He followed the same bookkeeping procedures that the previous owner had followed.

You can determine what quality of bookkeeper you have **(pages 93-96)**. Follow the steps at the end of the month. If any items on the balance sheet are not correct, your Income Statement may not be correct.

CONTINUOUS MONITORING OF THE NUMBERS

A referral from a drive-in grocery called me. After I arrived at the business and we went over his bookkeeping, I pointed out that the sales were over the limit for his bookkeeper's method of computing sales tax. Later he was audited by the state and owed a big tax bill. He called me again and I became his bookkeeper. Little did I realize that, over a twenty year period, he would buy and sell many businesses.

He would buy a business that was losing money. I would set up the bookkeeping so that he could look at the monthly financial statements and determine where the operating problems were. When I brought the statements, he would look over the numbers and ask questions, especially if he thought an amount was not in the normal range. After confirming the amount was correct, though abnormal, he would find out what caused it to be that way and make adjustments. Hence, almost all the failing businesses he bought were turned around and became profitable and were sold. What he did was what good mangers of retail businesses do.

The man's wife was a big part of his success, as wives are for many of my small businesses clients. Initially, I pointed out to them that their retail books were not set up to control cash. Her husband asked her if she would like to have the books set up for cash control and she did **(pages 147-153)**. When they bought a business, she set up necessary paperwork to control cash. She performed many of the functions of a comptroller competently even though she had no accounting knowledge and, at the beginning, no experience. **If a retail business does not control cash, the employees can steal without the owner knowing it.**

This man operated other types of businesses as well and was very successful. That is often not the case. He used the same principle of managing from his financial statements (Income Statement and Balance Sheet).

SUCCESSFUL BUSINESS PASSED ON

One day an entrepreneur called and asked me to stop by. I was his first and only bookkeeper. Little did I know then, as his first bookkeeper, that his business would grow from that small office and warehouse into one of the largest privately owned businesses, of that type, in Texas. It was interesting to watch his decision making over the years. He bid jobs at a certain profit for his service type business. Since the jobs required different rates, he looked to his Net Profit, rather than the Gross Profit, to see if the bid amount would enable him to reach his goal.

He kept doing something many entrepreneurs stop doing as their business grows: he did hands-on important office work. He bid all the jobs himself. He wrote all the vendor checks. He did the payroll for his increasing workforce, and he made all the deposits. He stayed attuned to his business and was very successful. The business grew tremendously over the years, expanding to several locations.

He was very wise in teaching his son about all facets of the business. Since his son took over the business, he has done a fabulous job managing the company. Being motivated and intelligent, he probably would have done well with no training, but his training and experience has given him a head start in running the business. He is astute in continually watching for new business opportunities to increase his income. His sister handles her responsibilities well, being in charge of the daily bookkeeping, vendor, and employee matters.

His son is now working following in his father's footsteps. At month's end, I do what is necessary to close the books, file any unfiled required reports, and take care of other matters. I report to the father and go over the monthly financial statements as I do with other business owners.

This company used to display a sign that read: *The only reason we are here is to serve the customer.* That is the reason the company has gotten top awards for outstanding service from Fortune 500 companies, etc.

An owner's heirs can ruin a business in a few months if they are inexperienced and are only interested in taking money out of the company, instead of making wise choices that enable the company to continue to be successful. It is very important that the owner train the family member taking over the business, provided someone wants to continue the work. Otherwise the owner could lose his investment in a short period of time if the heir squanders the company assets and doesn't take care of the customers.

HE DOES IT ALL

I had contacted a potential client. The full-time CPA, who had been doing the bookkeeping work for the company, had recently left. I explained to the owner that I could set up his bookkeeping in house on Peachtree Accounting software. I would train him to enter the data. He had no accounting experience at all. So I trained him, as I have trained many others, to do all the tasks on the computer necessary to successfully manage his business and have an accurate set of books. He is now amazed that he does all that work every day in a short time, since the CPA had done the same job full-time. He is also pleased that he can see the Total Sales and Net Income each day.

He has trained himself to be one of the best to handle problems in his specialty (particularly if the job is a big challenge). He is respected as having the expertise to complete any size job or very challenging jobs successfully by using his experience and his creative talents. **One way to maximize your profits is to become an expert in your field and do that type of work over and over.**

MANAGEMENT NUMBERS IMPORTANT:

SANDWICH SHOP

This business could not get enough sales to make an adequate profit for the time expended. The owner did everything to maximize the bottom line of her business. This illustrates the importance of keeping an accurate set of records. In order to make a profit, use those records, analyzing every cost and doing what is necessary to lower them, thereby lowering the total cost. That way you are making informed decisions.

Without a good set of books it is easy to get behind in paying taxes and in paying your suppliers. The tax agency can freeze your bank account and the supplier can make you pay for the products in full upon receiving them. Understanding your financial situation allows you to make your own informed decision to close or sell your business.

A Super Market owner decided to close one of his businesses when the sales, despite his best efforts and cost controls, did not provide the necessary profits. With accurate management financial statements, he was able to make an informed decision, thereby avoiding being forced out of business.

WHAT MIGHT HAVE BEEN

Here is one of the saddest stories in my many years of keeping books. I started doing the bookkeeping for a man after he had filed for bankruptcy. He had 2 million in sales the previous year and the jobs he worked should have provided a very good profit. He had two full time accounting employees, but no controls were in place. Since the books were not properly set up for management controls and financial statements were inaccurate, the actual financial situation was not evident.

There were a lot of vendor invoices, some paid and some not paid. We spent quite a bit of time figuring out what bills were still owed. After that was determined, he decided that he needed just one office worker. One employee quit and was not replaced. I set the bookkeeping up on accounting software and trained the remaining worker. The owner started getting a better picture of his business; it was showing a good profit. After a few years, the other worker quit and the owner's wife started helping with the bookkeeping. But things started to go bad when personal family problems hit. His wife found out she had cancer which resulted in her untimely death. Then he became ill for an extended period of time and finally died on the operating table.

That man never lost his faith and was always optimistic. It was a pleasure working for him, since I could be a real help. **What might have been**: If I could have set up his books before he had the 2 million in sales, he may have made lots of money. He would have had management oriented financial statements. The Income Statements would have shown deficiencies in his operations and, with his many years of experience, problems possibly could have been corrected.

The following 30 pages show you the inside pitfalls of operating a business as well as tips and other pertinent information.

The advice given is gleaned from years of experience providing bookkeeping and consulting services for many clients.

TIPS, PITFALLS,

AND OTHER INFO

Client stories with a lesson
Tips
Pitfalls to avoid

These many client stories illustrate the importance of what problems can arise that are not readily evident to the in-experienced business owner. Avoiding these pitfalls can greatly help avoid damage to their business.

Tips about different topics
General information is also given.

BUSINESS SUCCESS NOT LINKED TO EDUCATION

The owner's personal characteristics are most important.

Business success often does not require a certain level of education: especially in retail, construction, and many service businesses. High school drop-outs are very successful, as are college graduates.

Experience, good judgment, persistence, integrity, being aware of business pitfalls, an accurate management oriented bookkeeping system, knowledge of the cost structure, and understanding cash flow are the important factors in the success of most businesses. Understanding the financial statements enables businessmen to make timely decisions to correct the indicated problems. Various examples are given in this book.

Experience can be very helpful to avoid costly mistakes, to avoid situations that may cause problems. Experience teaches the entrepreneurs to promptly make a change when they realize a prior decision was a mistake.

Good judgment and leadership are needed every day. The ability to make good decisions and critical decisions is necessary. Do I hire this person or that person? Do I sell this new product? What should my price be, etc.?

Persistence is very important. Many problems surface when you start a business, especially when you are an under-capitalized beginning entrepreneur. **Success is the ability to keep going by focusing on the goal, rather than letting all the problems drag you down**. It is tough, if a customer doesn't pay, when you were depending upon his money to pay a critical bill.

These experiences work to make you a very good businessman for the long term.

If your cash or access to cash or credit is limited, it is very important to know what cash you have or will have and what bills are due now and which are due in the future – cash flow projection. Otherwise an essential bill, such as materials, might need to be paid when funds are not available.

Honesty in all dealings is very important when you are trying to increase your customer base and have loyal vendors. Vendors do not usually have much patience dealing with any businessman that has been dishonest with them. Customers of cheaters will complain to other customers about their bad experiences. Dishonesty is not healthy for the long term growth of the company.

A SIMPLE WAY TO STAY IN BUSINESS

Have enough cash or credit to pay essential purchases.

Always have enough cash or access to cash or credit to pay essential bills, etc. New entrepreneurs need to have, if possible, the least amount of personal debt and a less extravagant lifestyle when they start their business. The exception is if the husband or wife works outside the business to fund the personal liabilities and lifestyle, or if they are well capitalized.

A business with unlimited capital can learn from their mistakes and still stay in business. A business with limited capital does not have that luxury. That is the reason many business fail.

REDUCING PERSONAL EXPENSES TO STAY IN BUSINESS

Having less personal debt affords a longer time to achieve business success.

The personal car notes, other notes, credit cards, and lifestyle purchases you have to pay each month could affect your business's survival when part, or all, of that money has to come from the business.

It helps if married couples are in agreement about any lifestyle changes necessary to increase their chances of success in an undercapitalized business. Otherwise there can be tensions between lifestyle spending or using the funds to promote the success of the business.

If you want help in this area of reducing debt, a course provided by Dave Ramsey specializes in this and has been effective in showing many thousands of individuals how to reduce debt and stay out of debt. There may be other courses of this nature that are effective. Remember, the less cash you need to pay personal bills the longer your cash will last until you become a business success.

BUSINESS PLAN

Warning: Always watch projection of sales.

Overestimation of sales may be the number one reason for a business plan failure.

Many enterprising businessmen may start without a business plan. Because they are out of work and know a trade, they just start the business and make it work. However, for someone to quit their job and invest much capital into their business, it is very important to know if their decisions will work on paper. The idea still has to be executed.

I helped a client write a business plan for a new location. He was an energetic, personable person who knew his business and knew how to sell. When he told me what his projected sales would be, I had no idea if that estimate would prove to be realistic. He probably didn't either. His financier looked at the financial statements, the financial history of the original location, and the value of the owned real estate, etc. to make the decision whether to finance the new building and equipment. If the sales projection would live up to plan, he would make a lot of money. Even though the business became profitable, the actual sales numbers did not meet expectations.

Preparing a business plan has to do with projecting, to the best of your experience and ability, what you hope will happen in the future for your startup business or purchased business. When purchasing an existing business, there are years of history (usually tax returns, if on an Accrual Basis) to study. A good plan can be projected from that. A new startup business plan has to be realistic in terms of sales. The Gross Profit (Sales minus Cost of the Product Sold) has to be realistic also. With adequate research, the operating expenses can usually be accurately projected.

It is critical to have accurate monthly management oriented financial statements when you start a business. With the proper information, you can make necessary adjustments to hopefully keep your business plan on the right track. Otherwise, you may find out that there is not enough money to pay the bills.

If you have limited capital, make a business plan <u>for yourself</u> estimating ½ of the sales amount that you gave to your lender. Then plan ahead what you will do if you have ½ of the sales of the projected total amount. By doing this, you can be prepared to save your business if necessary.

HIRING RELATIVES

Are you aware that relatives can be a great benefit or a downer?

Hiring relatives can be the best or worst decision for your business depending on the work ethic, character, and responsibility of the employee.

I have watched employers hire relatives and have a very positive experience. The relatives cared about the company. They came to work on time and made decisions in the best interest of the company.

And I have seen hired relatives really cause problems. One company owner had a son who would not come to work on time. The owner put up with it but griped about it. Another owner's son did not come to work on time one day. He put him on the night shift for a period of time then returned him to the day shift where he was no longer late. Another owner had a brother working for him who caused him lots of problems. The owner's mother did not want her son fired. The owner deferred to her wishes and suffered continuous problems caused by his brother.

I learned lessons from these and many other similar situations. You never hire a relative that you can't fire. You lay down the ground rules (maybe in writing, what you expect), and indicate to that person that a violation of those rules can result in him/her being fired. Maybe that person should be told that it is not personal, but necessary to treat all employees alike. If you have a problem with a relative, confront it right away; maybe the relative's work/attitude will improve and he/she may work well for many years.

BUYING OR RENTING YOUR BUSINESS LOCATION

I was listening on the radio to a very successful investor and trainer who buys real estate for passive income (rental income). He proposes having enough passive income to pay your monthly bills so that you can retire at any time. That principle can also be helpful to a business owner who would buy a building rather than rent it.

Some businesses have to be in shopping centers or office buildings or warehouse buildings. However, those owners who build or buy a facility, have the opportunity to acquire passive income when they are no longer in business. They can rent out the building to the one who buys their business or to someone else.

It is important to do your best to buy in a location where property values will rise and to purchase the property at a reasonable price. After a 20 or 30 year period, you will have a valuable asset and possible passive income rather than those rental receipts.

PARTNERS FIGHT

What can happen when partnerships break up?

A unique situation came up a few years ago. Two business partners went to court to determine if, according to their agreement, one partner had the right to take controlling interest in the business. The court ruled in that partner's favor.

The business was the biggest in their industry. The partner who became subject to the other's authority set up another company. His company was well capitalized and the original company was not. The partner who lost the controlling interest underbid on contracts as they came up for renewal, and probably lost money but succeeded in taking the contracts away from his ex-partner. With less income and high fixed overhead, the original company went into Chapter 11 bankruptcy. The bankruptcy trustee required that I had to deliver reports by a certain date each month. I was impressed that you could tell at a glance that the reports accurately depicted the financial condition.

Though the original business operated for a while, the court closed it when it was determined the owner could not be successful in the future because the company was continuously losing contracts.

Who would have predicted that miserable outcome? From my experience, partnerships between friends or siblings very seldom work. But partnerships between mother/daughter or father/son often work.

DENTAL CROWNS & PARTNERHSHIPS

(a successful father/son partnership)

Another account was a company that made the crowns for dentists. It was amazing to see these plaster gums and teeth sitting around. The business was a partnership between a father and son. This family type of 50/50 partnership has the best chance of success, since they know each other's traits and are willing to work together. Most people do not realize that a 50/50 partnership between friends, or even siblings, will probably result in a broken relationship. "I did not realize that he/she was that way," is usually what you hear when they break up. When one partner owns more than 50% of the company, he can tell the other person what to do. If the minority partner doesn't like it, he has two options: put up with it or leave. That does not mean the other person is not a fine individual—he just believes in handling situations differently than you do.

If the 50/50 partnership goes out of business and the company does not pay incurred debt, either partner can be liable for all of it. For that reason partners should want to set up their company as another type of entity such as an LLC, S Corporation, Limited Partnership or even a C Corporation **(see pages 161-165)**. However, if the 50/50 partners guarantee the debt, they are still individually liable.

CONTRACT LABOR

Is your labor "contract labor" in the eyes of the IRS?

A few months after I started keeping books for a T.V. shop, it was audited by the Internal Revenue Service for work done in a year prior to my involvement. The auditor reclassified their listed contract workers as salaried employees. The owner was billed about $10,000.00 for the payroll taxes (social security plus withholding taxes) on these salaried personnel. When you pay legitimate contract labor, the employer does not deduct payroll taxes from the worker's check.

Though there are many factors determining whether a worker is considered an employee, the number one reason is the extent to which the owner controls the person's work. When you hire an electrician, you tell him what you want done in general terms and he figures out how to do it. And he works for many other companies. When you have an employee, you tell him how to do it. The laws have been liberalized, so check with your accountant about the current rules.

VERIFY BALANCE SHEET AND INCOME STATEMENT BEFORE BUYING A BUSINESS.

If you are buying a business or making a substantial investment in a business, you should verify that the Income Statement and Balance Sheet are correct, especially Inventory detail, Accounts Receivables detail, and Accounts Payables detail and any other substantial amount on the balance sheet. Also verify that the numbers on the Income Statement were derived using the Accrual Method **(pages 87-91)**; otherwise, the Income Statement might not show needed management information.

LEGAL MATTERS

Check legal contract before buying a business.

Another referral, who was buying a large store, called me. The owner had a Small Business Administration loan from a local bank, guaranteed by the government. He had acquired a business loan with a five year option to purchase. He was very successful. His wife kept the cash control detail that I set up **(see pages 147-153)**. When the five years had passed and he elected to purchase the business, there was a problem. The legal paperwork had not been correctly executed. The contract read that the buyer did not have the option to buy the business, but the owner had the right to sell it after five years. So he lost that store and all the hard work he and his wife had done to build it. It would have paid to have an outside attorney read the contract prior to signing.

LEGAL FEES

Legal fees can easily get out of hand when you do not know how to control them.

If it is a lawsuit, understand that most lawsuits are settled before they go to trial, often in arbitration. So there are pre-trial costs as well as court costs if your case goes to trial before a judge or jury. If you have limited funds, you may want to minimize the pre-trial costs so you have funds to take the case to trial, if necessary. To plan your pretrial and potential trial costs, try to get an estimate of such legal costs when you hire an attorney. Always get a detailed statement of work performed, not just the general: "for services rendered".

BUSINESS NETWORKING INTERNATIONAL (BNI)

How a business group can increase sales.

A personable moving company client invited me to a breakfast hosted by a network of entrepreneurs, of which he was a member. There are approximately 25 businesses represented in BNI. No two members cater to the same needs, so each member has a monopoly on any particular service that another member might use. Every member has to attend most of the weekly meetings or forfeit his membership. They each pay a yearly membership fee and a weekly fee for the meeting room and breakfast. Meetings begin at 7:00 a.m. All members take turns standing to briefly summarize what their business does. One entrepreneur, per meeting, gives a short presentation about his business. Then business cards are exchanged between participants as they let one another know of any service they can provide. For example: If someone needs a mover, he gives the job to the owner of the moving business. I was impressed that so many job opportunities were exchanged between members. And this happens every week.

I am not endorsing BNI, since I do not know the quality of the organization. Being a member of this or another networking group may not work for many businesses, but for the ones that do benefit, it can be very helpful.

NEW OWNER MAKING CHANGES

Are **major changes** necessary for successful business?

I got a referral call from a person buying a large store. He was very enthusiastic. The store he was buying was supposedly profitable. Rather than slowly changing its operation, he made lots of changes right away. He was not successful over the long term.

My judgment is that if the challenge you love is to make operations better on a big scale, you should buy a losing business. If you buy a successful business, it should be as an investment. It may be even better if possible, that no one knows there is a new owner so that customers don't critically compare your method of operation to the previous owner's way of doing things.

ACCESS PROBLEM

Will you have good road access to your business?

In 1972, I started keeping books for a drive-in grocery store. After this business opened, road workers began the long messy process of widening the street in front. His business was adversely affected with reduced sales.

When you consider buying or renting a business location, check with the county or city to determine if there are any street projects planned which would affect you and, if so, find out the projected time frame from start to completion.

BIG STORE COMPETITION

Are you subject to chain store competition?

If you want to start a business such as a grocery store where large chain stores are competitive, have a plan to compete if one opens close to you. Their purchase costs for products are probably lower than your purchase costs would be.

Two of my clients had individually owned large retail stores that were very profitable. A larger chain store, of their type of business, moved in causing their sales to drop substantially as profits turned into losses. (Overhead items such as rent and utilities often can't be reduced. If the level of sales cannot be maintained or increased over the long term, you may be out of business.) Happily, both were able to escape from their situation. One had a 10 year lease contract that was improperly written. He learned from that experience and later bought another business, negotiating for five two year leases. That way, he was only bound to pay 2 year's rent at a time and was not locked in for a longer period. My other client owned his building and was able to profitably rent it.

COMPANY TAKING CREDIT CARDS

Did you know that taking credit cards can increase sales?

I had a client who did not take credit cards for sales. One day a customer came in to buy his product, but didn't have the cash to pay and therefore did not purchase the product. The same scenario happened shortly afterward. The owner started accepting credit cards for payment. A few years afterward, about one half of his sales come from credit card payments. Credit card use might not work for all businesses, but it is true that customers, without cash, are willing to make a purchase on credit resulting in sales and more profit for many business owners.

TAXES

PAYROLL TAX DEPOSIT

Did you know that the IRS often voids the penalty for first time late returns or deposits?

An employee's withholding taxes and social security taxes **((B-2) page 61 & pages 69-70)** are taken from his gross pay; the employer matches the amount of social security taxes. Then the businessman follows certain rules for depositing taxes with the Internal Revenue Service. Failure to deposit these taxes on time results in penalties. Many business owners may not realize that if they inadvertently pay an Internal Revenue deposit late or file a business return late, the IRS will often void the penalty if the company has a history of paying on time (reasonable cause). The company may just send a letter stating that they have faithfully filed on time in the past, will continue to do so, and would like to have the penalty voided. Or they may indicate why the deposit or return was deposited or filed late. There is no certain way to respond. If they have been late in the past, the IRS usually won't void the penalty.

SALES TAX

Why is it so important to collect the correct sales tax?

New business owners often get into trouble paying their sales taxes since they may be due monthly, quarterly, or even yearly. Instead of setting aside the collected tax money, owners use it to pay other bills. When it is time to pay the tax, the money is already spent.

After a short duration, failure to pay sales taxes on time can result in your sales tax permit being suspended according to your state's collection policy, or your bank account may be frozen.

Not knowing the sales tax laws that affect your business, could cost a tremendous amount of money if you are audited. The sales tax is not applied to profit, but a certain rate is applied for each taxable sale. That amount of tax should be collected as part of the selling price; otherwise the accumulated uncollected amount could be much more than income tax. In Texas, an audit covers the last 4 years. In another state that length of time may differ. Where applicable, a sales use tax could also be due.

Find out what the sales tax laws are in your state before you open your business. Go to the sales tax office if necessary. You may be able to email questions to the state office if there is confusion about the taxability of any transaction.

UNEMPLOYMENT TAXES

Did you know laid off workers can increase an employer's tax rate?

These taxes are paid into a fund by the employer based on the wages of their employees. The rate is based on the amount drawn by laid off employees.

The owner had received a notice from the Workforce Commission but he did not open it. He filed the quarterly report not knowing what the notice said. The employer's rate went up to 8% of eligible payroll the next year. He had been notified that two of his ex-employees, who had quit, filed with the Commission claiming that they had been laid off. If he had opened the letter, he could have informed the agency of the deception and his rate would not have increased.

The amount of the unemployment benefit is usually based on the wage history of the employee and reason for termination. It is important to open letters from government agencies. Each state sets its own rules in regard to rates and salary amount subject to tax. Also, it is important to document all employee rule violations in case these records are needed for evidence at a hearing. That evidence could prevent your rates from increasing.

STATE CHARTER TAX

Do you know that you need to file an annual report?

To keep your corporation from forfeiting its state charter, the state tax report may need to be filed and the amount owed paid by a certain date. The charter gives you the right to conduct business in that state. Failing to file and pay the tax, if any is due, can result in your charter being forfeited and your corporation losing its separate entity for liability purposes. Then you are personally liable for all the corporation's liabilities. Check when the state tax report is due each year. You can often check the internet to determine whether your charter is in good standing after you have filed your return and paid your taxes, though the information can be misleading.

PAYROLL TAXES ASSESSED
TO OTHERS

How a secretary may be liable for all the company's delinquent payroll tax:

A client of mine had just opened his new business when he received a letter from the Internal Revenue Service assessing him company payroll taxes **((B-2) page 61 & pages 69-70)** not paid by his prior employer. Most people probably do not realize that the person who writes the checks can be held responsible for any unpaid taxes—even if that person is not the owner or part owner or, maybe, just has a secretary's position. To avoid being held responsible, do not be the one who decides whether to pay the IRS or another bill instead. In the case above, the man did not have anything to do with payments at his previous job so he was released from the obligation.

The penalties add up quickly if you fail to pay the Internal Revenue Service. If the company goes out of business or gets behind in paying taxes, the Internal Revenue Service can seize assets of any responsible party to cover the payroll taxes. Whenever a letter is received from the IRS, respond and set up a payment plan, according to their guidelines, if funds are not available. If you do not respond, a freeze may be put on your bank account and then other action taken.

ANNUAL INSURANCE AUDIT

How could the annual audit be wrong?

When you hire employees, you may have Workmen's Compensation insurance. That means that if they get hurt, the employer's insurance will pay for the employee's medical bills. The employer's annual salary amount is estimated to arrive at the annual premium. The owner pays a fixed rate per one hundred dollars of salary for each type of salary: office, field, etc. The employer can usually pay this premium annually or in monthly payments.

At the end of the year, the insurance company audits the salary figures and compares it to the estimated salary. If the salary figure was less than estimated, you get a refund. If it is more, you will have to pay the insurance company an additional amount.

The rate is based on how likely it is for the employee to get hurt. The office employee rate is very low, while other employees' rates may be much higher.

Insurance companies can give future rate decreases or discounts when your accident rate is zero or low. Those reductions can amount to substantial money when you have many employees.

BAD DEBTS

The business goal is to collect the debt and keep the customer.

Collecting bad debts is an art. Customers that fall behind in their payments have to be handled differently according to their type of business, the amount owed, their income level, and their future need of your product or service.

The goal is to collect the money for the past due amount without alienating the customer. The first thing to do is to make the payment due date clear to them. The second is often hard to put into practice and often a last resort with much consideration: Consider not selling to them or doing more work until you get paid for the past due amount, or work with them on some type of payment plan. The customer will say he is going to get a big check next week and will be able to pay you, but "next week" may be delayed or even never come.

This is where the art of collecting starts-- making a decision on how to get the money and still keep the customer. If he owes you a large amount of money and you anger him, you might not get any money and lose a customer. He may use the cash money he would have eventually paid you to pay a competitor to continue to get the product needed for his business.

A company with many Accounts Receivable balances can mail a past due notice after 30 days or after the payment date agreed upon. If the payment is not received after a short period of time, make a pleasant call to the past due customer. The customer will tell you when he is going to pay. If payment is not received by that day, call again. That puts the customer on notice that the seller expects to be paid by the due date. At this point, the customer will often pay you rather than another creditor, who is more lax in collecting, and you will still have his business.

Experience will teach you the best collection method for your business. Your situation might require action completely different than the advice given above. However, this principle is probably true in many cases: contact by mail or other means and continue follow up. Exercising patience and using your best judgment lets the customer know that payments are expected promptly. That is the art of collection.

YOUR CUSTOMER GOING INTO BANKRUPTCY

Is it economical to file a claim for debt owed you by a customer in bankruptcy?

It is often wise to fill out the paperwork, if the amount owed to you is substantial. You may not get any money, since other creditors may have priority over the available cash. It may take months or even years to get the amount owed to you. But you may be surprised. See what paperwork is involved and whether you can handle it without expensive legal help.

JAPANESE COMPANY
Business can sometimes fail quickly.

I became the bookkeeper for a Japanese company doing business in the United States. That was very interesting. The manager would add numbers on his abacus, doing it as quickly as someone using a calculator. The man was an excellent manager and had many accounts.

After a few years, the manager became dissatisfied that his pay was not being increased even though the financials were sterling. So he quit after a few years. The owners sent someone else over to manage the business. I did the Accounts Receivable records **((A-3) page 60 and 64)** for a while. Then, one day, the new manager called and said that they would be doing the work themselves. A year later I found out that the company had gone out of business; their Accounts Receivable records had become all screwed up and customers left. And they may not have mastered the art of collection.

Many entrepreneurs do not realize how critical it is to have accurate bookkeeping and good collection methods when they are buying and selling on credit. It is easy to keep good accounting records today with proper software and training and, if necessary, proper supervision.

THE BIG JOB

A big job can put you out of business.

I kept books for a company that did construction jobs for a few years. The new company was doing okay until the owner took a very big job. Things did not work out as planned. The job costs were greater than the quoted sales price. The costs were so much greater than income that the company was forced out of business. Often, bidding on big jobs is not worth the risk of losing your business, when you are inexperienced and/or capital is limited. You have to have extra money or credit to stay in business after losing money on a big job.

UPGRADING TECHNOLOGY

Is it possible to know when to upgrade technology?

Two main products are manufactured in this business, one of them being produced for many years. Due to the high quality of the products, the owner enjoys much repeat business. But, like all very successful businessmen, he is continually looking for ways to increase profits. He invested in two machines, costing about $400,000.00, that are able to do work many of his competitors cannot do. He makes a higher gross profit in this business than he gets from other business income. **Knowing when to buy machinery which incorporates new technology is important**. A good businessman does not buy on impulse; he weighs what he can earn in a normal economy against the cost of the equipment. A pitfall is that during a boon economy, some business owners, thinking the boon will last a long time, increase their overhead and debt. When the bust comes, they may find themselves loaded up with debt that can affect their survival.

DONATIONS

Find out how much of your donation goes to charity.

I gave a donation for a children's Christmas Party. Later, I found out that much of the donation went to the promoters. Since then, if I'm not familiar with the charity, I ask the solicitor to send their financial statements. Then I tell them I will read the statements and decide whether or not to make a contribution.

Many people might not know that some of the needy recipients get only a small percent of the amount collected for them. The charity's operators might think that giving *some money* to the needy is better than them having none. The Better Business Bureau or similar organization might be able to tell the percentage of the amount that actually reaches the charity.

THREE PARTNERS

Partners - Important for 3rd party to check accuracy of records

One company had three partners. The business would sometimes have a big profit one month and the next month a big loss. One of the partners blamed the fluctuation on my bookkeeping. I had the business manager partner give me the outstanding bills each month. My bookkeeping tied to that total. When a month's record's showed a big loss, we looked at the books and checked the dates of the invoices paid and accrued. It turned out that the partner paying the bills paid only some one month, showing a big profit. The next month, he would pay most of the money owed; the Income Statement would show a big loss. Thereafter, we never had that problem. **Any business partner can check whether that is happening (pages 87-91).**

BANK CALLED LOAN

Watch for contracts where the bank can call a loan even when payments are current.

Also during the 80's, a client got a call from his bank saying that his $100,000.00 loan **((B-6) pages 61 & 71)** had been called in. That meant he had to pay it in 30 days, even though he was current on his loan. He had the cash, so he paid it. I do not know what the law is today, but back then a bank could call in a loan when they felt insecure. Demand for full payment could be made at any time. When a bank holding company was buying many small east Texas banks, the big bank gave many business owners 30 days to pay off their loans, even though their payments were current, otherwise the collateral would be confiscated. A small east Texas independent bank had a highway billboard that read: "I call my banker Bill. What do you call yours?" Before borrowing from a bank, find out if there is any way you can be made to pay off the remaining loan amount with a 30 day notice even when your payments are current.

SELLING A BUSINESS WITH GOODWILL

A business without fixed assets often needs to be sold for cash.

I had a client that sold a business (much of its value was goodwill) and received half of the selling price at the time of the sale. The business did not do as well as expected and the new owner was not able, or not wanting, to pay the balance of the debt. So he hired an attorney to sue for fraud. Rather than go to court, the new owner and my client settled and paid for my client's attorney fees of $10,000.00 due to estimated trial costs equaling the amount owed.

Most cases are settled in arbitration where both sides try to settle the case before it goes to trial. Pre-trail legal costs in many cases should be minimized.

Selling "goodwill" means the buyer is paying for the business' accounts or customers above the value of the fixed assets and other assets that have value. The buyer of the business then has the benefit of not having to build his business from scratch and, in many cases, starts making a profit from day 1.

When the seller sells his "goodwill', he usually needs to get the full sales price at the close of the sale, unless the buyer has assets to use as collateral for the loan. Later, if the seller gets the business back because the new owner couldn't pay the note, he may find the business is worth a lot less now because good customer service was not maintained and the customers went elsewhere.

I had a client who sold a business for a huge amount of money that was an exception to the above. His note from the buyer was paid and the business increased because he sold it to a person whose character and experience were evident.

EXPANDING TO A SECOND LOCATION

I was surprised to find out that a certain food establishment was located in my area of town. I had driven by many times not seeing the sign which was in a strip center hidden by a corner building. I have learned that all the food they prepare is made on site from scratch, based on family recipes. Their business has grown by word of mouth without advertising.

They recently expanded to a second location. The business at the original location increased and the sales from the second location is quickly increasing. By consistently providing good food at a good price, they have established customer goodwill.

Deciding to open business at a second location requires a lot of forethought, planning, and commitment. At one location, you are there to handle daily problems and the employees are in place and are experienced. Opening a second location requires hiring a manager for the original place and having to train new employees. Getting sales to cover the overhead for the new location is a major problem to consider. An additional set of financial records has to be maintained. Of course, there are many initial problems to solve like: choosing the right location, the building or space satisfying your need and vision, dealing with the contractor, interior designer, paying fees and obtaining permits. It is a big challenge, but if successful, it can be very profitable.

LICENSES/PERMITS

Knowing what licenses or permits you need is important so that opening the business may not be delayed.

If an occupancy permit is required, you may need to bring the building electrical system, or whatever, up to code. If you buy or rent unaware of permit requirements, you could be required to spend thousands of dollars before the business can open. Depending on your type of business and location, you may need few or many licenses or permits.

A LONG TERM POSSIBLE PROBLEM FOR CASH STRAPPED BUSINESSES

A continuous cycle to avoid:

When the 1980s came, oil prices dropped to $10.00 a barrel. For many entrepreneurs, who had expanded their business thinking oil prices would hit $80.00 a barrel, it was a difficult time. Many lost their businesses; many people lost their homes. Anyone who has studied the economy over a long period of time knows that booms and busts happen in its various sectors. The responsibility of any businessman is to intelligently guess whether the present boom is temporary or long term. Making a correct assumption is sometimes hard to do. If the economy slows down, the problem of maintaining expanded overhead costs can cripple a company.

Business is good for a few or more years and then there can be downturns. **It is during these downturns that management decisions can affect future cash flow.** That is the reason to have accurate financial statements. They can illuminate whether you are losing money or decreasing your liquid assets such as cash, etc. or taking on more debt.

Often when a smaller undercapitalized business starts to lose money in a downturn, they delay paying their taxes (sales, payroll, and income taxes), and increase their credit card balances and notes payable amounts to stay in business. Then when business gets better, they pay all the past due taxes, credit cards, and notes payable. A business operating for years can repeat this process.

It is often hard to judge whether "business loss" or less-than-needed profit to pay bills is a temporary or longer term problem.

A business with accurate financial statements can try to cut as much expense and outgoing cash flow as possible when profit is less than anticipated. Since the future is uncertain, deciding when to do that is often a hard decision to make. But it is important to avoid the cycle of continuous debt increase during business downturns and debt decrease during business upturns. Increased profits could be saved rather than used to pay past due bills.

ACCOUNTABILITY

Management oriented financial statement - about accountability.

A supermarket may have three main departments: grocery, meat, and produce. If the sales for the grocery, meat, and produce departments are all recorded as one amount under Sales and all related purchases are lumped together under Purchases, there is no accountability for the heads of the meat and produce departments. However, if you record the meat & produce sales, purchases, and inventory separately to get a Gross Profit and Gross Profit % for those departments; you now have accountability. An owner can compare each actual Gross Profit percent against the projected Gross Profit percent. The department managers have do their best to meet Gross Profit projections, because now the boss knows what the numbers should be.

Figuring individual job costs is a way to have accountability for the service and parts/service businesses. The leader or leaders of the different jobs would manage the parts and labor costs to meet gross profit projections.

Successful businesses are very committed to accountability. Such discipline usually makes a business work smoothly. Small businesses normally do not have the many management layers of big corporations. Often the head of any small business department reports to the owner or maybe one person under the owner. When there is a management problem, it can be taken care of immediately rather than having to go up the chain of command and then maybe nothing happens.

DAILY CASH RECONCILIATION

The Daily Cash Reconciliation is very important for a business that receives cash for the sale of products or services, mostly a retail business.

The Daily Cash Reconciliation verifies the cash at the end of the day against the amount of cash you should have.

Retail businesses that don't use the Cash Reconciliation often fail. Employees realize that the owner does not know when cash is stolen.

Rather than doing this daily checkup sheet manually, larger businesses purchase a machine that handles all transactions and achieves the same purpose. However, machine numbers need to be monitored and verified.

DAILY CASH RECONCILIATION FOR BUSINESSES THAT RECEIVE CASH

The Daily Cash Reconciliation is probably the most important activity you can do if you own a retail business that handles lots of cash. It can keep employees from stealing your money. It allows you to determine whether <u>the cash you have on hand</u> at the end of day <u>equals the cash you should have</u> by doing the following. If the amounts are not close, you search for the reason.

RECORD: The beginning Cash at start of day

ADD: All sales whether cash or credit

ADD: Other receipts (payment of a returned check, rebates, etc.)

MINUS: Cash payouts - invoices, loans to employees, etc.

MINUS: Bank Deposits

MINUS: Credit card and other charges

The addition and subtraction above will equal <u>the cash you should have</u>.

Then count <u>the cash you have</u>.

The difference is your over or short cash amount.

Considering the many cash businesses that I kept the books for, very seldom was the Daily Cash Reconciliation over-or-short-amount equal to 0. However, very seldom was the difference great between the actual cash and the amount it should have been. A large difference could mean embezzlement.

Note that this is a manual format for a Daily Cash Reconciliation. You can achieve the same purpose on a computer spreadsheet or buy a machine that handles all the components of this spreadsheet.

By understanding the components of a Daily Cash Reconciliation, you will be able to audit your machine information.

An example of the Daily Cash Reconciliation is shown on the following two pages.

DAILY CASH CHECK UP SHEET OR CASH RECONCILIATION:

	3-29-14	3-30-14	3-31-14	Total
A) Sales	$5,450.34	$3,287.25	$4,535.63	$13,273.22

B) Receipts: Cash or Check or Credit Card

	3-29-14	3-30-14	3-31-14	Total
B1) Return checks re-deposited	$ 100.00		50.00	150.00
B2) Payment by Employees (on loans)	$ 100.00		25.00	125.00
C) Beginning Cash	$ 200.00	187.24	1,957.34	$ 2,344.58

D) TOTAL Receipts

	3-29-14	3-30-14	3-31-14	Total
	$5,850.34	$3,474.49	$6,567.97	$15,892.80

E) Payouts with cash:

	3-29-14	3-30-14	3-31-14	Total
E1) Purchases (by cash)	$ 700.00	500.00	235.00	1,435.00
E2) Employee Loans	$ 100.00			100.00

Sales payment not received:

	3-29-14	3-30-14	3-31-14	Total
E3) Credit Card Sales	$2,000.00	1,000.00	1,000.00	4,000.00
F) Deposits (taken from D)	$2,800.00		5,000.00	7,800.00

G) **TOTAL**
$5,600.00 $1,500.00 $6,235.00 $13,335.00

H) Cash to Account For
$ 250.34   1,974.49   332.97   2,557.80

I) Actual Cash Count
$ 187.24   1,957.34   387.24   2,531.82

J) Cash Over & Short
$ -63.10   -17.15   +54.27   -25.98

A) **Sales** are your actual cash, check, and credit card sales for the day--All Sales.
B) **Receipts** (Returned checks that were re-deposited and employee payments on loans are shown, etc.)
C) **Beginning Cash** is the ending cash for the previous day (I). Example: (C) on 3-30-14 $187.24 is the same as (I) on 3/29/14.
D) **Total** is the total of Sales and other receipts.
E) **Payouts with cash-** only what was paid out in cash goes here (E1-purchases & E2-employee advances).
  Note E-3 is credit card sales which are Credit Card Receivables; funds you will receive in a couple of days. That credit card deposit to your bank will wipe out this Accounts Receivable. However, enter the total credit sales on this date no matter when you receive payment. **Note that the payment of these credit card sales are deposited into a bank and entry made there to reduce these credit card sales receivables.**
F) **Deposits-** the money deposited in the bank, includes checks with the cash.
G) **Total** is the total paid out in cash including bank deposits and credit card sales.

H) Cash to Account For is the amount of cash you should have on hand (including checks). Subtract (G) Total from (D) Total.

I) Actual Cash Count is the total amount of cash & checks on hand at the end of the day or when the day ends for that cashier.

J) Cash Over & Short (Subtract I from H.)- If you have less cash (I) than you should have (H), something happened to the money. In my many years of doing the books for many supermarkets and other retail businesses, I have seldom seen the Over & Short be 0. However, for any month, the Over & Short amounts should offset so that the shortage or overage is minimal.

-

If the **Over & Short** is large one day, get your employee involved (if the employee's total is short) and spend much time trying to find out why. That should make the employee aware that you will not tolerate large shortages.

Note: As was mentioned in the discussion about sales **(page 52)**, this Cash Reconciliation will not detect when an employee does not ring up the sale. The book gives some remedies.

Also note that you, as an employer, should verify the numbers on the Cash Reconciliation by looking at the detail that supports the numbers: sales tapes, purchase receipts, return check names, employee's loan repayment, credit card totals, etc.

Doing the Daily Checkup Sheet is a lot of extra work. But without this information, your books may show profits when the cash is not there; employees might be stealing your cash.

Remember if yours is not a retail business and customers are billed, you normally do not need to do a daily Cash Reconciliation.

Accounting entry for the given 3 day operation for a retail business:

	Debit	Credit
Sales (A)		$13,273.22
Return Checks **(B1)**		150.00
Due from Employees **(B2)**		125.00
Purchases **(E1)**	$ 1,435.00	
Due From Employees **(E2)**	100.00	
Accounts Receivable		
Credit Cards **(E3)**	4,000.00	
Bank Account **(F)**	7,800.00	
Cash On Hand (3/31/14) **(I)**	387.24	
Cash On Hand (beginning 3/29/14) **(C)**	200.00	
Cash Over & Short **(J)**	25.98	
Total*	$13,748.22	$13,748.22

*Note: Debits always equal credits. If not, the books are out of balance.

The above might seem complex. Over the past 45 years, I have trained many people, who had no previous accounting knowledge, to do the Cash Reconciliation. With few exceptions, they did excellent work. One important point: If you do not do the Cash Reconciliation for one day, your books will be messed up. It may take lots of time to straighten them out.

Once you start cash reconciliation, you never stop.

JOB COSTS

Normally these are the bigger jobs and not retail.

Purpose of Job Costs is to know the material, labor, and overhead costs of each job so management can determine whether the profit results met its goal.

If not, management analyzes the bid price, material, labor, and overhead costs to determine if changes need to be made and what to change.

Management should be aware of a practice of transferring the extra costs of a job, which is over its projected cost, to another job. That does not help management judge the success of its projections. Your Job Cost work in that situation would be a waste of time.

Computers make it much easier to keep such records. However, the company needs to stress accuracy of entering the information into the computer program.

Management should not start a Job Cost program unless they are willing to insure its accuracy and will use it for management. Otherwise, it is extra bookkeeping costs for no benefit.

JOB OR PROJECT COSTS FOR NON-RETAIL BUSI-NESSES

Most Service and Service/Parts businesses do not use Job Costs. It takes extra bookkeeping and in many situations is not feasible. They use their overall Gross Profit %. If that is not adequate, they investigate.

However, the Job Cost information could be very valuable for management purposes. It shows which types of jobs are most profitable. You can also judge the efficiency of the employees involved.

Do the following:

Record the hours that each employee works on each job.

Record material costs for each job.

Record overhead items such as gas for transportation.

If you have many small jobs each day, it may not be feasible to keep these records with the bookkeeping involved, unless you have a good online computer system and can verify the accuracy of the information.

Make sure the job manager does not incorrectly allocate costs to another job when the amount exceeds the budgeted job's hours or cost. You need to have the correct information necessary to determine the reason for the cost overrun. True numbers are critical. For management purposes over a period of time, it helps to know which types of jobs are more profitable. When you know what type of jobs are most profitable, your salesman can try to sell more of them.

JOB COSTS DETAIL PROCEDURE

These are the costs when a workman:

a) goes to an individual residence or place of business and performs a service and sometimes provides material or parts to fix the problem or finish a project.
b) works on different projects at the customer's place of business.

The jobs' costs in either case are the labor costs of the workman and any material or parts used. The overhead such as insurance, uniforms, vehicle expenses, etc. can be divided among the different jobs by actual costs or by the company formula.

Procedure:
Each job is given a name and/or number.
Each hourly paid workman takes the number of hours x wage rate to equal his wages paid on each job.

Example:		**Job A**	**Job B**
John	30 hours x $15.00	$450.00	
John	10 hours x $15.00		$150.00
Sam	20 hours x $14.00	$280.00	
Sam	20 hours x $14.00		$280.00
Total		**$730.00**	**$430.00**

Payroll checks were written for work from March 1 to March 28. At the end of the month, they each worked March 29 & March 30, but were not paid until the following month.

	Job A	Job B
John	16 hrs. x $15.00 (Job B) 3/29 & 3/30	$240.00
Sam	16 hrs. x $14.00 (Job B) 3/29 & 3/30	$224.00

	Job A	Job B
Total Costs (Accrued Salary)		$464.00
Add: Total Job A & B Above not billed	$730.00	$430.00
Total Inventory-Labor-In-Progress	**$730.00**	**$894.00**

The job was not billed until April, so all cost was Inventory – Labor-in-Progress.

This amount ($730.00 + $894.00 or $1,624.00) would be shown on the Balance Sheet as Inventor-Labor-In-Progress.

It would then be applied to the jobs next month when billed.

The big benefit of Job Costs is that over a period of time you learn which type of jobs are the most profitable. Then you can market to those types of jobs.

When the project is on the business' premises, employee time and material is allocated to the project. You can give the foreman or supervisor the number of budgeted hours for each job. He should not allocate hours worked, beyond those budgeted, to other jobs. Also make sure that idle time is charged to idle time.

At the end of the month, you do the following:

1) Show the correct Accrued Salary Payable on the Balance Sheet. If the accrued salary was correct the previous month and entered correctly for the present month, the total salary will be correct for the present month.

2) Add together the total salary and material or parts costs to each job (can easily be done by an accounting program).

158

3) Add overhead cost to each job (either direct overhead, or % allocation of hours for specific job). Overhead costs are all costs, except material and labor, that pertain to that job. Example: cost of fuel for truck

Example: 17 hrs. for specific job/340 hrs. total overhead expense for all jobs = .05. $5,000.00 total cost of all jobs x .05 = $250.00 overhead for that 17 hour job.

4) The labor, material, and overhead costs = the Job Costs.

5) Subtract each job's costs (4) from the income for that job. If the job has not been billed, the costs are shown on the Balance Sheet as Inventory Labor-in-Progress. Then if the job is billed next month, those job costs are applied to the billed jobs.

6) Find the Gross Profit % of each job. This is very useful in directing your marketing to certain job types where the Gross Profit % is much bigger.

Example:
Job C billed:
Sale----------------------------- $1,000.00
Cost of Operation:
  Material $ 400.00
  Labor   300.00
  Overhead   100.00
  Total Cost of Operations $ 800.00

Gross Profit $ 200.00   20.0%

Today's accounting programs allow the numbers to be easily entered. Then you will be able to have a job profitability report **for each job.**

CHOOSING HOW TO ORGANIZE YOUR BUSINESS

Usually choose one of six legal ways to operate the business: Sole Proprietorship, Partnership, Limited Partnership, Partnership LLC, C Corporation, S Corporation

Each has its own liabilities and tax characteristics.

The rules below are general rules. Consult a professional before making a decision on the structure of your business. Congress could have changed the rules. Also there may be exceptions to the general rules shown below such as a S corporation election that has certain requirements.

THE USUAL SIX WAYS TO ORGANIZE YOUR BUSINESS

It is often hard to decide at the beginning which business formation is best, since what might be beneficial today might not be beneficial in the future, when profits are much greater.

TYPES OF BUSINESS ORGANIZATION AND THEIR CHARACTERISTICS:

Below are the detailed tax and liability characteristics for the 6 main types of business organizations.
1) **The sole proprietorship**
2) **General Partnership**
3) **Limited Partnership**
4) **Limited Liability Partnership (Partnership LLC)**
5) **C Corporation**
6) **S Corporation**

The type of organization you choose, in your particular circumstances, can make a huge difference in your tax liabilities and personal liability. You may want to discuss this with your accountant to find out which is best for you long term.

SOLE PROPRIETORSHIP
a.) Business owned by you
b.) Personally liable for any business debts
c.) Your business net income is added to other income on your personal return (entered on Schedule C).
d.) Both halves of self-employment tax (15.3% total) are paid (Schedule SE) on your personal return.

e.) You get to deduct ½ of the tax on your personal return.

GENERAL PARTNERSHIP

a.) Pay income tax on your share of the partnership income.
Receive K-1 schedule from partnership **for your share of partnership income** (including other tax items). Also included on Schedule E and maybe other schedules of your personal return.

b.) **BIG DANGER**--liable for all the debts of the partnership if partnership or any partners can't pay. Need to make sure partners have integrity, willingness, and capacity to share financial burdens if partnership fails.

LIMITED PARTNERSHIP

Limited vs. General Partnership:
Limited partners are not liable for partnership debts (unless there is a signed personal guarantee of debt payment). They are similar in most other ways.

LIMITED LIABILITY COMPANY (LLC)

a.) An individual owner LLC can elect to be taxed as a Corporation (Form 1120) **or** (1120 S) where the individual pays the tax. Otherwise he files on his personal return (Form 1040, Schedule C) Two or more persons can file a Partnership return (Form 1065) where the allocated income and other information is shown on the K-1 schedule that the partners use to file their personal tax returns.

b.) Individual is not liable for debts of the limited liability company (unless they signed a personal guarantee of any debt).
Assets of the limited liability company may not be subject to seizure by the winner of a lawsuit. See state laws.

CORPORATION (C Corporation)

a.) A regular corporation as a separate entity pays income tax on its net income: Form 1120.
b.) Like a limited partner, the owners (stockholders) are not liable for any business debts (unless a personal guarantee has been signed). Corporate assets may be seized by creditors after proper legal procedures.
c.) The stockholders pay income tax on the salary (W-2) or dividends (1099-DIV) received from the corporation, but not on the business profits.

CORPORATION (S CORPORATION)

a.) An S Corporation (Sub S Corporation) usually does not pay income tax on its income but files its income tax return on Form 1120S with attached K-1 schedules, also given to its stockholders. The stockholders then file the income and other items on their personal returns.
b.) Unlike a partnership, there is no self-employment tax on the amount of income shown on the K-1 schedule that is not salary.
c.) Like a C corporation or a Limited Liability company, stockholders are not liable for corporate debts (unless personally guaranteed by any stockholders).

COMMON CHARACTERISTICS:

Individual taxed rather than entity taxed
Sole proprietorship
General Partnership
Limited Partnership
Limited Liability Company (your decision)
Sub S Corporation

Entity taxed
Corporation (C Corporation)
Limited Liability Company (your decision)

Personal liability on entities' income
Sole proprietorship
General Partnership

No personal liability on entities' income
Limited Partnership
Limited Liability Company
Sub S Corporation
C Corporation

The choice of how to organize your business is based on your desired liability protection and potential income taxes for your level of income. Note: to keep liability protection, you usually need to file an annual state return separate from your state income tax return. See state tax laws.

a: CONVERTING INCOME FROM CASH TO ACCRUAL

Figuring income using the Cash Method does not give you an accurate bookkeeping record of what actually happened that month or period. When you file your first tax return with the Internal Revenue Service, you check the box: Cash or Accrual. The next tax returns have to follow the way you chose to file the first tax return, unless you get approval from the Internal Revenue Service.

The examples below are not about proper accounting entries to convert from Cash to Accrual Method. They are illustrations of how to figure your actual income (Accrual Method) before changing your Cash Method system over to the Accrual Method or verifying the correctness of your Accrual Method.

The examples below show how to verify that your accrual statements are correct by making sure that all of your income is what was earned that month or period.

Income on Cash Method converted to Accrual Method:

Income on the Cash Method is determined by invoices (bills to the customer to whom you sold products or services) including those invoices dated for the previous month(s) that are paid in the present month.

Invoices dated for the present month may not be included in Cash Method Income, when those invoices have not been paid.

For the Accrual Method, income should be only invoices dated for the month – in this case May.

Note that calculation converting from the Cash Method to the Accrual Method is tied to the following:

Earned and billed this month: **Accrual Method**

5-3-2017 invoice	$2600.00
5-20-2017	1400.00
5-25-2017	1300.00
5-27-2017	1200.00
Total Accrual Income	**$6500.00** (See next page

Using *the* **Cash Method** for the month of May, 4 deposits, totaling $7,500.00, were counted.

4-13-2017------$1500.00	5/2/2017
4-15-2017--------2000.00	5/3/2017
5-3-2017--------- 2600.00	5/20/2017
5-20-2017--------1400.00	5/27/2017
Total $7500.00	

All invoices dated any month but deposited this month-CASH METHOD INCOME

TO CONVERT TO ACCRUAL (Proof)

Cash Deposits in May------------ $**7500.00**

Subtract: Previous months billings
4-13-2017 deposit---$1500.00
4-15-2017 deposit---- 2000.00   **3500.00**

Add: May Unpaid invoices:
5-25-2017------------ $1300.00
5-27-2017------------- 1200.00   **2500.00**

Accrual Income------------------- $**6500.00** (Previous page)

b: CONVERTING PURCHASE & OPERATING COSTS FROM CASH TO ACCRUAL

Purchases on Cash Method converted to Accrual Method:

Using the Cash Method, purchases are only recorded when paid, similar to income recorded on the Cash Method.

Having your accounting system on the cash method can result in very misleading income statements.

Your business or organization thinks that the financial situation is good when in reality many bills may not have been paid.

Proof:

5-3-2017	$400.00
5-20-2017	600.00
5-26-2017	1400.00
5-31-2017	1300.00
May 2017 purchases	**$3,700.00**

On a **Cash** basis, you have the following invoices recorded for the month of May.

4-27-2017	$500.00
4-29-2017	500.00
5-3-2017	400.00
5-20-2017	600.00
Total Paid	**$2,000.00 Paid in May**

In this example, May showed $2000.00 purchase cost using the Cash Method but $3700.00 using the Accrual Method.

To convert to Accrual:

Total paid in May----------- $2,000.00

<u>Subtract</u>: previous month's purchases
4-27-2017	500.00
4-29-2017	500.00 - **$1,000.00**

<u>Add</u>: unpaid bills at end of month

5-26-2017	1400.00	
5-31-0017	1300.00	**$2,700.00**
Total purchases		**$3,700.00 (previous page)**

<u>SUMMARY</u> SKELETON VIEW OF BUYING OR STARTING A BUSINESS

The following pages are a sketchy progression of buying or starting a business and its subsequent operations. (Many terms discussed here have been previously covered in detail.)

As I have mentioned before, if you want to hands-on manage your business, immerse yourself with the information in this book. Learn its principles.

Planning cash flow before buying or starting a business
Before buying or starting a business, it is important to access your personal cash flow and what impact implementing your plans will have.

Having ample cash when you start or purchase a business can often result in quicker success. You don't have to use a lot of time to plan how to pay bills as they become due. Also you can bid a normal price. An undercapitalized business may bid a lower price to get the job to pay bills or, in the case of a retail business, sell at a lower gross profit to generate cash.

The successful undercapitalized businessman continually monitors his cash flow. Adequate cash flow is necessary to be able to pay bills. For the non-retail business, the two main factors in planning a positive cash flow are: (1) know when your customer is supposed to pay and (2) know when you need to pay your bills. Planning what to do when a customer does not pay on schedule is very important.

When a business is undercapitalized, personal debt, business debt, and overhead expenses put an owner in a position where more time is required to manage, to make plans to get the needed funds. Often to avoid extra cash flow outlays, the businessman may buy used fixtures and equipment, pay lower rent in a poorer location, use a credit card only for essential purchases, and keep the same vehicle he has until his profits allow him to afford another one. However some businesses require an upscale image to be successful and therefore have to initially spend more on overhead.

But every situation is different and every business profit structure is different. Each owner uses his own skills, judgment, and experience to overcome disadvantages. You can't say one underfunded business will be less successful than another with debt. However, you can say that the chance of success is often greater for a business, with limited capital, that has lower overhead and debt.

Checking financial statements before buying a business
If you are buying a business, it is important to know how accurate the bookkeeping statements are. Getting copies of previous tax returns can help. However, if the taxes were prepared on a Cash Method rather than an Accrual Method, as explained previously **(pages 87-91)**, the tax return is not likely to be an accurate assessment of the profitability of the business. As mentioned before, it is often necessary to do your own investigation. Inventory can easily be increased, based on no evidence, to increase the net profit figure, etc. After determining the statements are correct, that there is enough profit and/or potential, and enough cash flow (if your cash and access to credit is limited) a decision to buy that business can result in a very valuable purchase.

Advantage of buying a business

The advantage of buying a business is that customers are established and that you can, to an extent, project your sales. When starting a business from scratch, projecting sales is very hard to do. Those entrepreneurs often get themselves into financial trouble by making a business plan that overestimates sales. Such businessmen can help themselves by making bare bone cash outlays until the business becomes profitable. If you are buying a non-retail business, it is also very important to look at the Accounts Receivable, Accounts Payable, and Inventory if any. Fake Accounts Receivables, understatement of Accounts Payable, and overstatement of Inventory give an inaccurate perception of increased income.

Many businesses are started on a shoestring after the individual loses his job. Those businessmen, often by necessity, have to continually manage their cash flow in order to live and operate the business until they earn ample cash. They have to exercise all of their creativity to make the business successful. These owners get lots of experience managing cash flow; their businesses can become very operationally efficient and successful because the owner did what was necessary to stay in business.

Cash or accrual basis for your bookkeeping

After you own the business, you determine whether to keep your records on a Cash or Accrual Method. For management purposes, the bookkeeping is usually always on the Accrual Method **(pages 87-91)**. You can convert bookkeeping to the Cash Method for tax purposes. You shouldn't make a decision to buy or not to buy a business based on tax returns figured on the Cash Method.

In-house or outside bookkeeper

In many cases to properly manage the business, you will need to have your bookkeeping in-house or hire an outside bookkeeping service. The outside bookkeeping service could set up your bookkeeping in-house, train the individual keeping the books, and help close the company books at the end of the month to ensure that they are accurate. This book showed how to check up on the accuracy of your bookkeeper's financial statements. Just because your bookkeeper is competent does not mean that your statements will accurately present the information you need. The bookkeeper employee might do sloppy work with inadequate oversight. You can read the information in this book to monitor your bookkeeper **(pages 93-96)**.

Being your own bookkeeper
An owner or his wife may not realize that either can easily become a full charge bookkeeper even though they do not have the skills of an accountant. The owners will learn how to bill their customers, make deposits, enter vendor invoices, write checks on the computer, and do computer payroll. This is all easy to do when the individual is a detail person and has patience. I have a client who never finished high school who does excellent work performing all the steps mentioned above. By learning this, the owners will know how to get financial information from the computer at their whim. Managing the business this way may be much easier. A non-service business requires a little more teaching. I don't remember ever training a business owner who did not do a good job. However, it usually takes a 50 year old longer to learn than a 25 year old! The outside bookkeeper can answer any questions during the month and close the books at the end of the month.

Looking at your numbers to manage the business
This book went into detail about many facets of looking at numbers to manage your business; so this is very brief.
If you own **a retail business**, it is particularly important to have a correct Gross Profit number **(pages 27-33)**. A correct Gross

176

Profit means the Sales, Cost of the product and Inventory numbers are correct. If you own **a non-retail business** that bids jobs, the profit will vary from job to job. Hence these businesses often look first at their Net Profit. If it is not adequate, they investigate their bidding process and the cost of doing the work. They, like the retail business, also look at all the Operating Expenses to determine whether the purchases are wise and proper.

Make sure that every item on the balance sheet is correct. Don't be afraid to ask for a bank reconciliation, Accounts Receivable and Accounts Payable Aging Schedule, and the makeup of any other item of the Balance Sheet. Those reports should equal the Balance Sheet total. If an expense item was put on any total on the balance sheet or was improperly accounted for, the Income Statement is incorrect.

Managing your Cash and Accounts Receivables
If you have bought a cash business (like a grocery store or bar) or you start a retail business from scratch, it is very important to use the Daily Cash Reconciliation **(pages 147-153)**.

Failure to do that can result in employees being tempted to steal cash; it also fosters error in figuring the Gross Profit Percent. A non-retail businessman usually bills his customer. Often, the bigger his customer's business, the slower that customer pays. Small business operators often pay right away while a large business operation might wait 90 days to pay. An undercapitalized business owner may pay his workers every week and pay his suppliers within 30 days. He could be in big financial trouble if he has to wait 90 days to get paid. He might have to postpone doing work for a big client unless he can negotiate with that customer to pay more promptly.

Image

When a new business starts, money is often spent for *image.* That is important when image is critical to your type of business. However for many new customers, price and service are the most important factors in gaining their loyalty. Until you are making sustainable profits, cash outlays may be made only for necessities to avoid getting into a cash bind.

Perseverance

"Perseverance" is a big factor in success. It means to keep managing the business with correct numbers even when the business is struggling. This is the time for creative management to kick in. After you come through that trying experience, you will probably be a very successful entrepreneur. You probably will not be afraid of failure from then on.

If you are in business:

Remember: Monitor your business.

Remember: Persevere.

Remember: Keep a positive attitude.

Remember: Every failure you have is an experience. Many successful businessmen have lots of experiences.

Remember: Get as much information as you can from other entrepreneur's experiences.

Remember: You can be a successful businessperson whether you are a high school dropout, high school or college graduate, or a PHD. However, it is an enormous help to know your business and follow the operational principles in this book.

Remember: Always prepare the Income Statement and Balance Sheet on the accrual method so that correct numbers are available to manage the business or organization.

Your notes:

www.ingramcontent.com/pod-product-compliance
Lightning Source LLC
Chambersburg PA
CBHW060607210326
41519CB00014B/3590